T0313417

"*The Reformed Pastor*, by the preeminent pastor-theologian of the Puritan era, Richard Baxter, is one of the first books I read on the Christian ministry. As a pastor, I need to read and reread this classic. Crossway and Tim Cooper have done a great service to the church in making this updated and abridged volume available to us. May God use this book to save and care for many souls through pastors in his church."

Mark Jones, Pastor, Faith Vancouver Presbyterian Church; coauthor, *A Puritan Theology*

"In the history of pastoral life, certain books stand out as classics that must be read by anyone who is serious about this utterly vital sphere of the Christian world. One immediately thinks of the books on pastoralia by Gregory the Great or Martin Bucer. Among this select group is Richard Baxter's *The Reformed Pastor*. It can be a daunting read, for Baxter demands much of anyone who would seek to serve as a pastor to the souls of men and women and children. Daunting though it is, it is a must-read. For here we find not only a book that has influenced generations since it was first published but a work that sets forth the high calling of being a minister of the gospel. The latter is not in vogue today for a number of reasons, and to some extent we are reaping the fruit of our failure to highly prize pastoral leadership. May the reading of this new edition, rightly abridged, serve to rekindle among God's people a prizing of the pastorate and a prayer for those who serve in it. May it be a key vehicle to help refocus the passions and goals and energies of those currently serving as shepherds of God's people!"

Michael A. G. Haykin, Professor of Church History and Biblical Spirituality; Director, The Andrew Fuller Center for Baptist Studies, The Southern Baptist Theological Seminary

"*The Reformed Pastor* rightfully carries the description of a 'classic work in pastoral ministry.' John Wesley and C. H. Spurgeon both testified to its benefit in their lives and ministries, as have thousands of other pastors. Baxter scholar Tim Cooper has abridged Baxter's lengthy work into a more manageable (yet no less powerful) charge to pastors. It is my joy to commend this book to the current generation of ministers, that by carefully taking heed to themselves first, they will be better prepared to take heed to the flock of God."

Timothy K. Beougher, Associate Dean, Billy Graham School of Missions, Evangelism and Ministry; Billy Graham Professor of Evangelism, The Southern Baptist Theological Seminary; author, *Richard Baxter and Conversion*

The Reformed Pastor

The Reformed Pastor

Richard Baxter

Updated and abridged by Tim Cooper

Foreword by Chad Van Dixhoorn

CROSSWAY®

WHEATON, ILLINOIS

Library of Congress Cataloging-in-Publication Data

Names: Baxter, Richard, 1615–1691, author. | Cooper, Tim, 1970–, other.
Title: The reformed pastor : updated and abridged / Richard Baxter, Tim Cooper ; foreword by Chad Van Dixhoorn.
Description: Wheaton, Illinois : Crossway, 2021. | Includes bibliographical references and index.
Identifiers: LCCN 2020022760 (print) | LCCN 2020022761 (ebook) | ISBN 9781433573187 (hardcover) | ISBN 9781433573194 (pdf) | ISBN 9781433573200 (mobipocket) | ISBN 9781433573217 (epub)
Subjects: LCSH: Pastoral theology—Early works to 1800.
Classification: LCC BV4009 .B3 2021 (print) | LCC BV4009 (ebook) | DDC 253—dc23
LC record available at https://lccn.loc.gov/2020022760
LC ebook record available at https://lccn.loc.gov/2020022761

Contents

Foreword

OF ALL THE PURITAN BOOKS that have cried out for abridgment, none has done so more loudly than Richard Baxter's *Reformed Pastor*.

Every pastor, not just Reformed pastors, ought to read what Richard Baxter has to say about ministry. In fact, I have never mentored an intern or taught a class on pastoral ministry in which I have not assigned some parts of Baxter's book for reading and discussion. But it has always been *some* parts. I think I am right in saying that I have never assigned the book as a whole. I have always required reading some of this and some of that, for Baxter is not consistently helpful, and he repeats some of the best bits more than once. He wrote a passionate appeal for shepherds to care for their sheep, but like many great pastors, he could not be both passionate and concise at the same time.

The main theme of *The Reformed Pastor* is the Christian minister's need for a personal pastoral ministry. In Baxter's England there were lonely people, sick people, and complicated families. There were Christians facing sin and suffering who lacked the assurance that they should have had. And there were churchgoers with a strong sense of assurance that they should not have had. Some of these people could be reached through powerful preaching. But not all of them. Thus, Baxter emphasized personal pastoral care for its own sake: a divinely appointed means, practiced by the apostle Paul himself (Acts 20:20), to bless the people God has placed in a minister's life. Not to give it all away, but Baxter's recipe for personal care includes praying, teaching, risking awkward questions, and insisting on hard conversations.

Baxter is most famous for his commitment to visitation. Visitation is a dying art in our day, but it need not die out altogether. Raising the topic of visiting families or individuals in a modern church is likely to raise eyebrows for most elders: "You want to visit every family in the church once a year?" It raises heart rates when elders in cooperatively shaped ministries discover that their pastor wants them to try it too: "You want me to *join* you on a visit?" And then, "Now you want me to do this by myself?" Of course, visitation is scary for members too: "Why does the pastor want to visit me? What did we do? Does he *know*?"

I remember trying to get traction with pastoral visits. I asked the secretary to set up meetings: her communications were ignored. I sent long emails with biblical explanations of why I'd like to visit: I'm not sure they were even read. I asked people after worship services if I could come by some evening to visit: panic and embarrassment. Then I started emailing a mixed group of people in the church (the alleged "problems" and the alleged "successes" in the same email) offering dates when I'd be available and telling them all I'd like to come and pray with them: success! The trial and error was painful for everyone but worth it, and I would never have persevered if it were not for reading Baxter and being persuaded by his driving concern that shepherds spend time with their flocks, that physicians of souls check in on their patients, that pastors plan visits with their people.

For what it is worth, Baxter did not press for private ministry because he was a poor preacher. As the wonderful introduction to this volume relates, there were points when Baxter's church was full to the point of bursting. But like any godly minister, he was wise enough to know that personal pastoral care enhances a public ministry. Knowledge of one's flock and of one's neighborhood enables the preacher to shape and apply sermons with maximal effectiveness. What is more, hearers notice when a minister is so committed to them that he will leave the security of his study and venture into the messiness of their lives. People are more likely to listen to people who love them—and who take pains to prove it.

Many Christians have wanted an abbreviated version of Baxter's classic. Tim Cooper finally took it into his hands, and he is the perfect person to do so. The introduction to this volume speaks for itself, but as an award-winning teacher, thoughtful Christian, and Puritan scholar, Professor Cooper has few rivals when it comes to Baxter. He has followed Baxter's footsteps by coediting the great man's autobiography.[1] He has so engaged the pastor of Kidderminster's theological and practical writings that he is able, if I may use the phrase, to think his thoughts after him. Dr. Cooper is the guide we have wanted, and the Christian world owes him a debt for this service.

In assigning sections of Baxter's *Reformed Pastor*, I always felt like I was coming to the text with a cleaver, butchering the book by assigning chunks here and there. Dr. Cooper has approached his task with a surgeon's knife, giving the book the slimmer look that some volumes need. In this case, when sewn back together, the effect is impressive. But the improvements include supplements too, such as introductions to chapters, questions for reflection, headings for orientation, and Baxter's own catechism as a guide to pastoral care.

---

1   Richard Baxter, *Reliquiae Baxterianae: Or, Mr. Richard Baxter's Narrative of the Most Memorable Passages of His Life and Times*, ed. N. H. Keeble, John Coffey, Tim Cooper, and Thomas Charlton, 5 vols. (Oxford: Oxford University Press, 2020).

Even though he admitted that it was longer than it needed to be, the Reformed pastor who first told me to read *The Reformed Pastor* also told me to read the whole thing. He was not unkind; he simply noted my personal deficits and knew that I would need every practical encouragement that Baxter (or anyone else) had to offer. I confess that I eagerly look forward to gifting him a copy of this expert abridgment. He now trains pastors himself, and my guess is that he now assigns to his students only the best selections of Baxter. I am also guessing that he, like me, will be happy to commend this fine abridgment instead.

Chad Van Dixhoorn
Westminster Theological Seminary

Introduction

WHEN RICHARD BAXTER PUBLISHED *The Reformed Pastor* in 1656, he had no idea that he had produced a classic text, one that would still be in print nearly four centuries later. The book was his exposition of Acts 20:28: "Take heed unto yourselves and all the flock, over which the Holy Spirit has made you overseers, to feed the church of God, which he has purchased with his own blood." His enduring work sets forth a vision of what pastoral ministry should be in all its rounded fullness. It summons pastors to tenacious, intentional, and sacrificial soul care of every individual under their oversight. The call is demanding and provoking, inspiring and affirming. If there is any one book that every pastor should read, this is it.

But be warned: it is no easy book to read. Partly that comes from Baxter's message, one that is uncompromising in its high call and expectations. Reading *The Reformed Pastor* is an uncomfortable experience, and in this abridgment I have made no attempt to soften that discomfort. In several other ways, though, I have tried to make the book a great deal easier to read, mainly by modernizing much of Baxter's seventeenth-century language and by reducing its length from 160,000 words to 30,000 words.[1] It is possible that in this concentrated

---

1   Any reader seeking a much fuller abridgment should read Richard Baxter, *The Reformed Pastor*, ed. William Brown (repr., Edinburgh: Banner of Truth, 1989).

form, Baxter's message is only more excruciatingly intense, focused, and demanding. The easier it is to access, perhaps, the more uncomfortable his book becomes.

I have, then, tried to make *The Reformed Pastor* much more easily accessible without diluting its force. It comes to us from a distant age; Baxter's words and vision may still carry that sense of foreignness. For exactly this reason, he can speak what we need to hear. His text, now centuries old, can expose the gaps in our own conception of what it means to be a pastor. We do not need to agree with everything he says, but long after his life came to a close, Baxter still speaks. More than ever before, his is a voice we need to hear.

Baxter's Voice in His Context

Richard Baxter (1615–1691) was an English pastor and a prolific author: *The Reformed Pastor* is just one of around 140 books that he wrote. On December 4, 1655, he planned to gather with his fellow pastors in the county of Worcestershire to commit themselves to a new way of ministry. As it happens, he could not attend. Dogged by ill health throughout his life, he found this to be just one more occasion when infirmity hindered his travel. Yet his preparations were not without fruit. It was his way to write out his thoughts in full, not only to do the best job he could of serving his fellow local ministers but also to share his ideas more broadly, with an eye to possible publication (he always sought to wring the greatest possible benefit from his work). And so it was. In the summer of 1656, *The Reformed Pastor* made its first appearance.

At that point, Baxter was in the middle of a flourishing pastoral ministry. But if we go back to April 1641, when he first arrived in Kidderminster at the age of twenty-five, the conditions did not bode well. Kidderminster was a town that had long been known for its weaving and cloth industry. It lay on the banks of the River Severn in the Midlands, about 130 miles northwest of London and around 40 miles from the border of Wales. Baxter's parish comprised the town itself along with twenty villages in the nearby surrounds, with a combined population of between three and four thousand souls. A parish is what formed the basic administrative district of the Church of England, which comprised around nine thousand parishes. When Baxter first settled in his new parish, England was drifting ever more rapidly toward civil war between Parliamentarians and Royalists. Four years of armed conflict on British soil began in October 1642, the outcome of rising tensions over constitutional powers, individual liberties, taxation, and, above all, religion. King Charles I sponsored a church style that emphasized deference and order, favored the sacraments over preaching, and unsettled a previous consensus that was broadly Calvinist in its doctrine. These changes tended to bring the Church of England closer in practice and doctrine to the church of Rome. For many, this was too close for comfort. Would England see the Protestant Reformation through to its conclusion, or would that cause go backward?

We might ponder for a moment that word *reformation* and its companion *reformed*, which anchors the book's title. During the sixteenth and seventeenth centuries, various reformations took place across Europe. For all the differences between them, the general aim was to re-form the church. For the most part, this meant bringing the church back to its initial shape in the time of the apostles as laid out in the pages of the New Testament and laying aside the worship and governance of the church that had become only ever more elaborate and even further removed from scriptural precedent across the intervening centuries. Therefore, a reformed church was one that resembled that first original. A "reformed pastor" was one who likewise followed the New Testament precedent. We might use the later language of "revival," which implies not just faithfulness to the scriptural model but a lively, energetic, sincere, and heartfelt minister and ministry. For Baxter, all this meant imitating the example that the apostle Paul laid out in his last speech to the Ephesian elders in Acts 20:18–35. Baxter's point is implicit but obvious: any reformation of the church must begin with a reformation of its pastors.

There was little reformation to be seen in Kidderminster in 1641 and little prospect of it. How that changed! The war took Baxter out of Kidderminster for several years, but after he returned in May 1647, now aged thirty-one, he once again set about his work in earnest. When he began, only about one family on each street comprised faithful, godly Christians. By the late 1650s, Baxter classed around a third of the adult population as consenting church members and visibly sincere Christians. Among the eight hundred families in the parish, he explained in a letter in 1658, six hundred adults were consenting church members. At first he numbered his converts "as jewels," but he quickly began to lose count, and five galleries (forming a second tier of seating layered above the first) had to be added to the parish church to accommodate his growing Sunday morning congregation.[2] This remarkable turnaround says much about Baxter's commitment, skill, and tenacity as a pastor. It is worth saying that he was unmarried. He believed it preferable for ministers to remain single so that they

---

2   Richard Baxter, *Reliquiae Baxterianae: Or, Mr. Richard Baxter's Narrative of the Most Memorable Passages of His Life and Times*, ed. Matthew Sylvester (London, 1696), 1.84–85, §136.

could devote themselves wholly to the work of ministry (see p. 84). He eventually married Margaret Charlton, one of his parishioners, but only in September 1662, after he had been ejected from public ministry; they never had children.[3] Thus Baxter threw everything he had into the cause.

Promising signs had emerged by March 1653, when, as Baxter explained in a letter to a friend, he considered himself to be "in the very beginning of a reformation."[4] He was starting to see clearly the kinds of structures needed to bring about a renewal of orthodox, scriptural, practical, sincere, and dedicated Christianity, and he was beginning to put those structures into practice. In doing so, he was taking advantage of a new environment. Since the execution of King Charles I in January 1649, England had ceased to be a monarchy. It was now a republic (or commonwealth) with power residing in the parliament and council of state. Oliver Cromwell, a member of the council of state and, from 1654, Lord Protector, became increasingly influential. More important, the Church of England had been legally (if not entirely in practice) disestablished. Parliament could not agree on any national ecclesiastical settlement to take its place, so the 1650s offered unprecedented freedom to experiment at the local level.

Baxter was a great experimenter. In his parish he matched effective preaching with the conscientious practice of confirmation (ensuring that those coming of age adequately understood and owned the

---

3 For an excellent introduction to their marriage and to the book that Baxter published after Margaret died in 1681, see J. I. Packer, *A Grief Sanctified: Through Sorrow to Eternal Hope; Including Richard Baxter's Memoir of His Wife's Life and Death* (Wheaton, IL: Crossway, 2002).

4 Richard Baxter to Richard Foley, March 19, 1653, Baxter Correspondence, vol. 4, folio 141r, Dr. Williams's Library.

Christian faith) and church discipline (based on Matt. 18:15–17, the process of bringing known sinners to repentance and, in the absence of repentance, excluding them from the church community). More widely, Baxter engineered the Worcestershire Association, a local network of like-minded ministers seeking to implement effective pastoral practice. They gathered together once a month to encourage each other, to discuss difficult issues, and to embody unity and concord at a time of division even among committed Christians. In 1653, and in their name, Baxter published *Christian Concord: Or the Agreement of the Associated Pastors and Churches of Worcestershire*. It declared their public resolution to perform the work of pastoral ministry and to undertake effective church discipline. Only those who consented to come under that discipline would be subject to it—that is, only those who intentionally adopted membership in the parish church and who declared their assent to the profession of faith incorporated in *Christian Concord*. This implied a direct conversation between the pastor and each consenting member of the parish, which meshed nicely with the fundamental resolve that "each minister should endeavor to know (if possible) each person in his charge."[5]

This public declaration in *Christian Concord* made no mention of a practice that Baxter began to implement around the same time. He was inspired by the apostle Paul, who taught both "publicly" and "from house to house" (Acts 20:20), but he had long been deterred by the sheer labor involved. How did one pastor possibly find time to meet individually with every person in a parish the size of Kidderminster? Baxter found a way. First, he employed an assistant. Second, they

---

5 Richard Baxter, *Christian Concord: Or the Agreement of the Associated Pastors and Churches of Worcestershire* (London, 1653), Propositions, sig. A3v.

each took all Monday and Tuesday every week to spend one hour with each family in the parish going through a catechism to gauge their understanding and practice of the faith. This catechism was a brief document of fundamental questions and answers designed to be easily memorized (see appendix 1 for Baxter's catechism, along with two suggestions for contemporary catechisms).

It is important not to underestimate the cost. He took a full two days out of each busy week to do this work. Touchingly, he later described how the very poorest families of the parish would come to him for instruction, leaving a "plentiful" supply of lice to inhabit his chamber "for a competent space of time."[6] His new system demanded dedicated, painstaking, careful work. Preaching, he discovered, was not enough to bring about the reformation he sought. It also required these one-on-one, individually tailored conversations. But the work paid off. Baxter felt he had hit on the decisive method to bring about a true reformation. As he declared in his preface to *The Reformed Pastor*, "We never took the best course to demolish the kingdom of darkness till now."[7]

In this way, Baxter pursued a reformation at Kidderminster from the ground up. Genuinely excited by the results, he glimpsed the potential of a countrywide movement that would see his method replicated thousands of times over in England's many parishes. He began to pursue this national vision with his fellow ministers in Worcestershire. That gathering in December 1655 was his opportunity to persuade a receptive audience to join him in this new work and commit

6 Richard Baxter to Thomas Lambe, September 29, 1658, in *Reliquiae Baxterianae*, ed. Matthew Sylvester, appendix 3, 63.

7 Richard Baxter, *The Reformed Pastor* (London, 1656), preface, sig. (a6)v. As in the abridged text, I have modernized the language in all the quotations in this introduction.

themselves to the practice of annual family visitations. In 1656, they declared their commitment (and published the brief catechism they would use) in *The Agreement of Diverse Ministers of Christ in the County of Worcestershire for Catechizing and Personal Instruction*. When Baxter published *The Reformed Pastor* that same year, it was his invitation to England's ministers to follow suit. As his confidence rose, he allowed himself to imagine a reformed England populated with reformed parishes overseen by many thousands of reformed pastors.

But it was not to be. Oliver Cromwell died in September 1658. The rule of his son Richard collapsed in May 1659, and the country slipped into chaos. A year later, the monarchy was restored, along with the bishops. The terms required for ministry in the restored Church of England were so narrowly defined that around two thousand ministers could not in good conscience comply. The bishop of Worcestershire refused Baxter permission to preach in Kidderminster ever again or even to offer a public farewell to his beloved parishioners. By 1662, Baxter's optimism had collapsed in the dust of bitter disappointment and reversal. Many years later, in 1684, he admitted that all these events had "made so deep a wound in my heart, as never will be fully healed in this world."[8] *The Reformed Pastor*, therefore, emerges from a context of excitement and optimism that ended all too soon. But it was written by a man who, if nothing else, had certainly put his own advice into practice—and to great effect.

Baxter's Voice in Our Context

All that history is important because it locates Baxter in a particular time and place, facing very real difficulties and obstacles. He was

---

8 Richard Baxter, *Catholic Communion Doubly Defended* (London, 1684), 7.

clearly a pastor who thought deeply about his ministry and was prepared to work hard to be effective in it. Yet his context could scarcely be more different from our own. In his day, people rarely moved or traveled. Most remained within the same parish their whole life. There was by definition only one church in each parish, so people had precious little choice about which church they attended. Back then, it was much easier to know exactly who was a consenting member of each parish and who was not. In our day, in contrast, people are nothing if not mobile. Each Sunday morning they might drive past ten or twenty churches to reach the one that best meets their needs or suits their preferences. They choose from a bewildering array of alternatives, and if they come to dislike the church they are in, they can easily move on to another one just around the corner. This makes it challenging for us to match the practical way that Baxter set about his vision of pastoral ministry.

There is also another crucial difference. These days, churches generally do not use anything like a catechism for intentional, individual instruction. Discipleship tends to be practiced in small groups, without the direct involvement of the pastor. Having read Baxter's prescription, we might ask ourselves if we have lost something important. Is it time we recovered the catechism or something like it?

Yet for all the substantial differences, Baxter's text remains powerfully relevant. Church members still require individual soul care as far as is possible, and the high values and biblical imperatives that drive Baxter's vision are timeless. Paul's speech to the Ephesian elders is still in our Bible. The human heart is fundamentally unchanged across the centuries, and Baxter's insight into the patterns of sin, grace, and the gospel remain lively and all too accurate. He was an extremely shrewd observer of his own heart as much as anyone else's, and his words of caution and encouragement for pastors remain both vital and current.

One reason Baxter's voice is so important is precisely that he *does* come from a context so different from our own. This is indicated on the title page of *The Reformed Pastor* in two obvious ways (see fig. 1). First, the correct title of the book is *Gildas Salvianus*. This is an allusion to two earlier figures in church history: Gildas the Wise, a sixth-century British monk, and Salvianus, a fifth-century French priest. Both men were remembered for speaking hard truths to their respective clergy. Thus, Baxter was co-opting an ancient tradition of calling ministers to account, which is why *Gildas Salvianus*, to give the book its proper title, is not always comfortable reading. Baxter was acutely aware of this. In his long preface (not included in this abridgment), he explained why he concentrated so much on the sin of England's pastors. The December 1655 gathering was, he said, first of all a day for confession and repentance. "The fire is already kindled that reveals our sin," he said, so why would they try to hide or deny their sin?[9] "Judgment must begin at the house of God" (1 Pet. 4:17). Effective leadership begins with candid self-assessment:

> I think it is no time now to neglect our duty and befriend our sins, and so provoke the Lord against us. Instead, it is fitting for us to fall down at the feet of our offended Lord and to justify him in his judgments, and freely and penitently to confess our transgressions, and to resolve upon a speedy and thorough reformation before wrath breaks out upon us, which will leave us no remedy.[10]

9 Baxter, *Reformed Pastor*, preface, sig. A3v.
10 Baxter, *Reformed Pastor*, preface, sig. A4r.

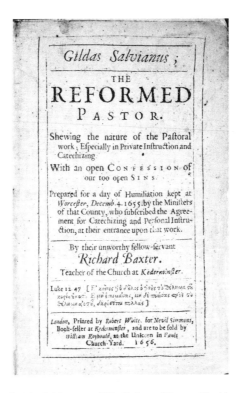

Figure 1   Original title page of *The Reformed Pastor*. Used by permission of Dr. Williams's Library, London.

Duty, sin, judgment, penitence, confession, wrath: these are not words we easily or usually hear. Yet Baxter confronts us with exactly this, for our own good and for that of the church. As the examples of Gildas and Salvianus show, "plain dealers are always approved in the end, and the time is at hand when you shall confess that those were your truest friends who spoke the hardest truths."[11]

11   Baxter, *Reformed Pastor*, preface, sig. (a3)r.

The second feature of the title page is a verse rendered (not unusually) in the original Greek from Luke 12:47. There are many verses that we might expect to see on the title page of a book for the encouragement of pastors today, but this is not one of them: "That servant who knew his Lord's will and did not prepare himself or do what was required will be beaten with many stripes." Baxter's choice of verse demonstrates again his acute concern for sin and judgment. Certainly, his God is a God of grace and love, but he is also a God who judges, who is displeased by sin in his children, and who expects from ministers that they lay down their lives for the flock.

This is not a particularly therapeutic Christianity, and yet, arguably, it speaks to the real condition of the soul and to the true nature of pastoral ministry. We might see all this as a touch dark and obsessive. Indeed, Baxter's perspective is, like anyone's, open to critique. But to the extent that sin, judgment, and repentance are underplayed in contemporary Christianity, his perspective and his voice become all the more important. He addresses a blind spot in our own way of seeing. Even if he speaks of judgment and sin too much, we speak of it too little. Let Baxter's voice, then, be heard again.

Baxter's Voice in This Abridgment

The Reformed Pastor presents the reader with a significant challenge: it is very long. My main aim, therefore, has been to make the book shorter. Much shorter. In this abridgment it is less than one-fifth of its original length. I have cleared away a great deal of material that I think the twenty-first-century reader does not need. I have removed those sections that relate to controversies of Baxter's day along with references to other writings from the seventeenth century or from further back in church history, as well as several long quotations in Latin. If

Baxter has already made his point earlier, I have sought to minimize repetition. If I have felt that he has made his point sufficiently in the first half of a long paragraph, I have quite happily omitted the second half, or I have retained what I think are the most pertinent, affecting, and accessible of his sentences and deleted the rest.

I have, therefore, taken liberties without making any of them obvious in the abridged text. I have reorganized the chapters. I have split many long sentences in two; amended Baxter's heavy use of colons, semicolons, and commas; modernized his rather random placement of apostrophes; and used contemporary spelling. I have inserted new words to ease the flow from one sentence to another or shifted a clause from the end of a long sentence to the beginning. I have also amended all those tiny archaic constructions that snag the eye and get in the way, removed the initial capital letter in many of the nouns, and replaced unfamiliar, ancient words with their contemporary equivalents. And I have modernized seventeenth-century verb endings (e.g., *hath*, *hindereth*). (See fig. 2 for a glimpse of Baxter's writing from a page in the original.) Even so, there is a residual strangeness to his writing. His distinctive construction of written English is a useful reminder that, for all the many continuities, Baxter lived in a world far different from our own. For the same reason, I have also not updated his gendered language.

In all this, my intention is to make the text clear and accessible. I want to offer you, even in this abridged form, the genuine Baxter. I have tried to be faithful to his original vision and purpose, as I understand them, and to convey what I think he would want to say to us now. I have tried to leave nothing out of the full text that is essential. I am seeking to relay his seventeenth-century message to a modern audience. I hope that it comes through cleanly, accurately, and powerfully and that you find you can read the text with relative ease.

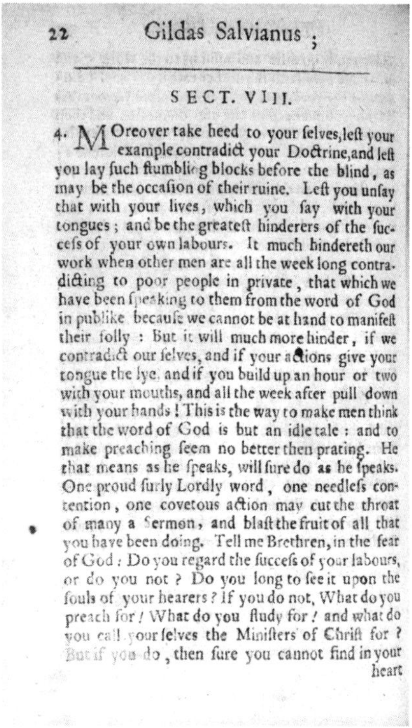
22 Gildas Salvianus ;

SECT. VIII.

4. MOreover take heed to your ſelves, leſt your example contradict your Doctrine, and leſt you lay ſuch ſtumbling blocks before the blind, as may be the occaſion of their ruine. Leſt you unſay that with your lives, which you ſay with your tongues; and be the greateſt hinderers of the ſucceſs of your own labours. It much hindereth our work when other men are all the week long contradicting to poor people in private, that which we have been ſpeaking to them from the word of God in publike becauſe we cannot be at hand to manifeſt their folly : But it will much more hinder, if we contradict our ſelves, and if your actions give your tongue the lye, and if you build up an hour or two with your mouths, and all the week after pull down with your hands! This is the way to make men think that the word of God is but an idle tale : and to make preaching ſeem no better then prating. He that means as he ſpeaks, will ſure do as he ſpeaks. One proud ſurly Lordly word, one needleſs contention, one covetous action may cut the throat of many a Sermon, and blaſt the fruit of all that you have been doing. Tell me Brethren, in the fear of God: Do you regard the ſucceſs of your labours, or do you not? Do you long to ſee it upon the ſouls of your hearers? If you do not, What do you preach for? What do you ſtudy for? and what do you call your ſelves the Miniſters of Chriſt for? But if you do, then ſure you cannot find in your heart

Figure 2 A page from the original publication of *The Reformed Pastor*. For the equivalent text in this edition, see pp. 33–34. Used by permission of Dr. Williams's Library, London.

It helps that Baxter is a great writer. He has a passion that infiltrates just about every sentence. He has a way of bringing in illustrations and metaphors from everyday life. You may notice his favorite images of the pastor: schoolmaster, soldier, and, above all, physician. These represent domains of life that shaped his own experience profoundly. Baxter is a very personable writer, willing to give himself away and to inject his own personality and intensity into his books. As William

Bates put it when he preached Baxter's funeral sermon, "There is a vigorous pulse in his writing that keeps the reader awake and attentive."[12] May the concentrated vigor of this abridgment keep you awake as well.

The Reformed Pastor is an extended exposition of one verse in particular, Acts 20:28: "Take heed unto yourselves and all the flock, over which the Holy Spirit has made you overseers, to feed the church of God, which he has purchased with his own blood." The English Standard Version renders this as follows: "Pay careful attention to yourselves and to all the flock . . ." Pay careful attention! First to yourselves, then to all the flock. The first chapter examines how we are to pay careful attention to ourselves; the next two chapters set out the way we are to pay careful attention to all the flock individually. Chapters 4 and 5 offer a confession of pastoral sin and a failure to pay careful attention. The next three chapters seek to motivate the reader by laying out the need, benefits, and difficulties for the work of individual pastoral instruction. Chapter 9 strongly rebuts six possible objections to Baxter's practice. The final chapter presents his practical direction and advice. All this takes us to the heart of the pastoral vocation. The book elevates our ideals. It sets a high bar.

Is it too high? *The Reformed Pastor* is inspiring and invigorating. It is also daunting and, potentially, discouraging. It is, almost literally, a recipe for burnout: "What is a candle made for but to be burnt? Burnt and wasted we must be" (p. 121). You will see that Baxter was driven by a perpetual sense of urgency. He is a physician living in a time of plague; a teacher of students whose final exam is, at any moment, just a heartbeat away; a pastor whose parish includes hardened sinners

---

12 William Bates, *A Funeral-Sermon for the Reverend, Holy, and Excellent Divine, Mr. Richard Baxter* (London, 1692), 112.

hurrying on to judgment. In the pages of this book, he is consumed by an overriding passion. He presents an ideal that only the most energetic and dedicated among us can ever hope to emulate. Therefore, this is a book that we must read, but we must read it with care. Be inspired but not burdened. Glimpse success, but do not feel defeated or despairing. Even if we do not match his standards, we can lift our own, and that can only be good.

In the book, Baxter was speaking to his fellow ministers, whom he addresses as his "brethren." He was speaking to them; now he is speaking to us. I hope his words are of interest to all those who take their Christian faith seriously, but in framing my brief opening summary of each chapter and in posing questions for reflection, I have in mind in particular those who are themselves in pastoral ministry (or who are preparing for it). That was me, some time ago, so I am not without experience. But I must admit that I still struggle to answer the question put to me by my good friend Robin Taylor, who so kindly read the first draft of this abridgment: "What do you want people to do with it?" An excellent question. What do we do with Baxter when we have largely lost the use of a catechism and the imminent urgency that invests his language of hell and judgment? We hear his call, but how can we possibly live up to it? That is the challenge of this book.

Even though the message is a difficult one to receive, let alone put into practice, I still believe it is one we need to hear. *The Reformed Pastor* remains a classic text, and it deserves to be read by a new generation of pastors. If nothing else, we need to know that those who have labored before us had a different view and different standards from our own. So I do have an answer to my friend's question, or at least an encouragement. Begin with Scripture, especially with the passage that so animated Baxter: Acts 20. This is one reason why I have tried to provide a reference for each of his allusions to the Bible: you can then assess for yourself the degree to which he has authentically grounded his vision in Scripture. Imitate the Bereans. When they heard the confronting message of Paul and Silas, they returned to the Scriptures afresh "to see if these things were so" (Acts 17:11 ESV). Follow Paul's advice to test all things and hold fast to what is good (1 Thess. 5:21). More than that, read through the book with others. That first gathering in December 1655 was a gathering of many. In Baxter's model, the pastor worked in a solitary parish, but he did not work in isolation. Gather other pastors or wise counselors around you to find the balance, perspective, and accountability you need. I hope the questions for reflection at the end of each chapter help with this.

Let Baxter speak. Hear him again. Put his vision into practice in your own time, in your own place, and according to your own values, capacities, and convictions. His pastoral labor came to an end in the distant past, but may his voice inspire and bless you as you fulfill your pastoral labor in the present day, for the good of "the church of God, which he has purchased with his own blood" (Acts 20:28).

Tim Cooper
Dunedin, New Zealand

1

Take Heed unto Yourselves

In this chapter Baxter offers four reasons for the importance of Paul's
command to the Ephesian elders to "take heed unto yourselves." He
then offers eight reasons why this is so critical to effective ministry.
The essential problem is the deceitfulness and stubborn staying power
of indwelling sin. Just as it can subvert the heart of any believer, it
is still at work in the hearts of pastors. They must pay close attention
to themselves.

———

IF THE PEOPLE IN OUR CHARGE are to teach, admonish, and exhort
each other daily (Col. 3:16; Heb. 3:13), no doubt we may do the same
for one another. We have the same sins to kill and the same inner
workings of God's grace to be enlivened and strengthened as our
people have. We have greater works to do than they have and greater
difficulties to overcome, so no less necessity is laid on us. Therefore,
we need to be warned and awakened as well as they do, and we should
deal with one another as plainly and intimately as the most serious
pastors among us do with their flocks. Otherwise, if only our people
have the benefit of sharp admonitions and reproofs, only they will be
sound and lively in the faith. I need no other proof that this was Paul's

judgment than his rousing, heart-melting exhortation to the Ephesian elders in Acts 20: a short sermon but not quickly learned. If the leaders and teachers of the church had thoroughly learned this short exhortation, how happy it would have been for the church and for them! Therefore, let us consider what it is to take heed unto ourselves.

The Importance of Taking Heed unto Ourselves

1. Take heed unto yourselves lest you be void of that saving grace of God that you offer to others and be strangers to the effectual workings of the gospel you preach. Take heed unto yourselves lest while you proclaim the necessity of a Savior to the world, your own hearts neglect him and you miss out on an interest in him and his saving benefits. Take heed unto yourselves lest you perish while you call on others to take heed of perishing and lest you starve yourselves while you prepare their food. Can any reasonable man imagine that God should save men for offering salvation to others while they refused it themselves and for telling others those truths that they themselves neglected and abused? Many a tailor goes in rags who makes costly clothes for others. Many a cook barely licks his fingers when he has prepared for others the most costly dishes. Believe it, brethren, God never saved any man because he was a preacher, nor because he was an able preacher, but because he was a justified, sanctified man and consequently faithful in his Master's work. Therefore, first take heed unto yourselves so that you will be that which you persuade your hearers to be, believe that which you persuade them daily to believe, and have heartily accepted that Christ and Spirit whom you offer unto others.

2. Take heed unto yourselves lest you live in those actual sins that you preach against in others and lest you be guilty of that which you daily condemn. Will you make it your work to magnify God and,

when you have finished, dishonor him as much as others do? Will you proclaim Christ's governing power and yet treat it with contempt and rebel yourselves? Will you preach his laws and willfully break them? If sin is evil, why do you live in it? If it is not, why do you dissuade men from it? If it is dangerous, how dare you venture upon it? If it is not, why do you tell men that it is dangerous? If God's threatenings are true, why do you not fear them? If they are false, why do you trouble men needlessly with them and put them into such a state of fear without cause? Do you know the judgment of God that those who commit such things are worthy of death (Rom. 1:32), and yet will you do them? You who teach another, do you not teach yourself?

3. Take heed unto yourselves that you are not unfit for the great employments that you have undertaken. He must not be himself a babe in knowledge who will teach men all those mysterious things that are to be known in order to enjoy salvation. Oh, what qualifications are necessary for the man who has such a charge on him as we have! How many difficulties in theology to be opened! How many obscure texts of Scripture to be expounded! How many duties to be done wherein ourselves and others may miscarry if they are not well informed in the matter, end, manner, and circumstances! How many sins to be avoided, which cannot be done without understanding and foresight! What manner of people ought we to be in all holy endeavors and resolutions for our work! This is not a burden for the shoulders of a child. What skill does every part of our work require, and of how much importance is every part?

4. Take heed unto yourselves lest your example contradict your doctrine and you lay stumbling blocks before the blind that may be the occasion of their ruin. Take heed unto yourselves lest you deny with your lives that which you say with your tongues and so be the greatest

hinderers of the success of your own labors. This is the way to make men think that the word of God is merely an idle tale and to make preaching seem no better than prattling. He who means as he speaks will surely do as he speaks. One proud, surly, lordly word, one needless disagreement, one covetous action may cut the throat of many a sermon and destroy the fruit of all that you have been doing.

Tell me, brethren, in the fear of God, do you value the success of your labors, or do you not? Do you long to see it in the souls of your hearers? If you do not, why do you preach? Why do you study? Why do you call yourselves ministers of Christ? It is a palpable error in those ministers who will allow such a distance between their preaching and their living that they will study hard to preach exactly and yet study little or not at all to live exactly. All the week long is little enough time for them to study how to preach for an hour, and yet one hour seems too much to study how to live all the week. They are loath to misplace a word in their sermons or to be guilty of any notable blemish (I do not blame them, for the matter is holy and weighty), but they make nothing of misplacing affections, words, and actions in the course of their lives. Oh, how carefully have I heard some men preach, and how carelessly have I seen them live!

Certainly, we have very great cause to take heed what we do as well as what we say. If we will be the servants of Christ indeed, we must not be tongue servants only. As our people must be doers of the word and not hearers only, so we must be doers and not speakers only, lest we deceive ourselves (James 1:22). A practical doctrine must be practically preached. We must study just as hard how to live well as how to preach well. We must think and think again how to compose our life as well as our sermons so that both may encourage men's salvation in the best way that they can. When you are preparing what to say in a sermon, you will always ask, "Which way should I lay it out for the greatest good, especially to men's souls?" You should ask the same question concerning the money in your purse. Oh, that this were your daily study: how to use your wealth, your friends, and all you have for God, as well as your tongues. Then we should see fruit for your labors that is never likely to be seen otherwise.

Why We Should Take Heed unto Ourselves

Having showed you in four particulars how it is that we must take heed unto ourselves and what is included in this command, I will now give you the reasons for it, which I entreat you to take as motives to awaken you to your duty.

Reason 1. You yourselves have a heaven to win or lose. You have souls that must be happy or miserable forever. Therefore, it concerns you to begin at home and to take heed unto yourselves as well as unto others. Preaching well may succeed to the salvation of others without the holiness of your own hearts or lives. It is possible at least, though less likely. But it is impossible that preaching well should serve to save yourselves. "Many will say to me in that day, 'Lord, Lord, have we not prophesied in your name?'" They will be answered with "I never knew you, depart from me, you who work iniquity" (Matt. 7:22–23).

Oh, sirs, how many men have preached Christ and perished for lack of a saving interest in him? How many who are now in hell have told their people of the torments of hell and warned them to avoid it? How many have preached of the wrath of God against sinners who are now feeling it? Oh, what sadder case can there be than for a man who made it his very trade and calling to proclaim salvation and to help others attain it—after all that to be himself shut out! Alas, that we should have so many books in our libraries that tell us the way to heaven, that we should spend so many years in reading those books and studying the doctrine of eternal life, and yet after all that to miss it! All because we preached so many sermons about Christ while we neglected him, about the Spirit while we resisted him, about faith while we did not heartily believe, about repentance and conversion while we continued in the state of flesh and sin, and about a heavenly life while we remained carnal and earthly ourselves. Believe it, brethren, God is no respecter of persons. He does not save men for their clerical clothes or callings. A holy calling will not save an unholy man.

Reason 2. Take heed unto yourselves, for you have a depraved nature and sinful inclinations as well as others do. If innocent Adam needed to take heed unto himself and lost himself and us for lack of it, how much more need have such as we? Sin dwells in us even when we have preached much against it. Alas, even in our hearts as well as in our hearers there is an averseness to God and a strangeness to him, along with unreasonable and almost unruly passions. In us there is at best the remnants of pride, unbelief, self-seeking, hypocrisy, and all the most hateful deadly sins. Does it not then concern us to take heed? Alas, how weak are those of us who seem strongest! How apt we are to stumble over a mere straw! How small a matter will cast us down by enticing us to folly or kindling our passions and inordinate desires, thus perverting our judgments, abating our resolutions, cooling our zeal, and dulling our diligence. Ministers are not only sons of Adam but sinners against the grace of Christ as well as others. Those treacherous hearts will one time or another deceive you, if you do not take heed. Those sins will revive that now seem to lie dead. Your pride, worldliness, and many a noxious vice will spring up that you thought had been weeded out by the roots. It is most necessary, therefore, that men of such infirmities should take heed unto themselves and be careful in the feeding and nurture of their souls.

Reason 3. Take heed unto yourselves, because such great works as ours have greater temptations than many other men face. Smaller strength may serve for lighter works and burdens. But if you will venture on the great undertakings of the ministry; if you will lead on the troops of Christ against the face of Satan and his followers; if you will engage yourselves against principalities, powers, and spiritual wickedness in high places (Eph. 6:12); if you will undertake to rescue captive sinners and to fetch men out of the devil's paws: do not think that a heedless, careless minister is fit for so great a work as all this. If you think that you can do such work as this with a careless soul, you must expect greater shame and deeper wounds of conscience than if you had lived a common life. It is not only the work that calls for heed but the workman also, that he may be fit for business of such weight. If you will venture into the midst of the enemies and bear the burden and heat of the day (Matt. 20:12), take heed unto yourselves.

Reason 4. Take heed unto yourselves, because the tempter will make his first or sharpest onset on you. If you will be the leaders against him, he will spare you no further than God restrains him. He bears the greatest malice against those who are engaged to do him the greatest mischief. As the devil hates Christ more than any of us, because he is the general of the field and the captain of our salvation, so does he hate the leaders under him more than the common soldiers. He knows what a rout he may make among the rest if the leaders fall before their eyes. Therefore, take heed, for the enemy has a special eye on you. You will bear his most subtle insinuations, incessant temptations, and violent assaults.

As wise and learned as you are, take heed unto yourselves lest he deceive you. The devil is a greater student than you and a nimbler disputant. He can transform himself into an angel of light to deceive (2 Cor. 11:14). He will get within you and trip up your heels before you are aware. He will play the conjurer with you undiscerned and cheat you of your faith or innocence, and you will not know that you have lost it. Indeed, he will make you believe your faith is multiplied or increased when it is lost. You will see neither hook nor line, much less the subtle angler himself while he is offering you his bait. They will be so fitted to your temper and disposition that he will be sure to find advantages within you and cause your own principles and inclinations to betray you, and whenever he ruins you, he will make you the instrument of your own ruin.

Oh, what a conquest will he think he has won if he can make a minister lazy and unfaithful, if he can tempt a minister into covetousness or scandal! He will glory against the church and say, "These are your holy preachers: you see what their scrupulousness is and where it will bring them?" He will glory against Jesus Christ himself and say, "These are your champions! I can cause your chief servants to abuse you. I can make the stewards of your house unfaithful." Oh, do not so far gratify Satan. Suffer him not to use you as the Philistines did Samson, first to deprive you of your strength and then to put out your eyes, and so to make you the matter of his triumph and derision (Judg. 16).

Reason 5. Take heed unto yourselves, because there are many eyes on you, and many will observe your falls. You cannot miscarry and the world not hear about it. If you take yourselves to be the lights of the churches, you should expect that men's eyes will be on you. If other men may sin without observation, you cannot. You should thankfully consider how great a mercy this is, that you have so many eyes to watch over you and so many people ready to tell you of your faults. In these ways you have greater helps than others, at least for the restraining of your sin. People may tell you your faults with a malicious mind, but you have the advantage from it. God forbid that we should prove so impudent as to do evil in the public view of all and to sin willfully while the world is gazing on us!

Reason 6. Take heed unto yourselves, for your sins have more heinous aggravations than other men's. You are more likely than others to sin against knowledge, because you have more knowledge than others. You know your Master's will, and if you do not do it, you will be beaten with many stripes (Luke 12:47). Your sins have more hypocrisy in them than other men's because you have spoken against those very sins. Oh, what a heinous thing it is to study how to disgrace sin to the utmost and make it as odious to our people as we can and, when we have done all that, to live in it and secretly cherish that which we openly disgrace!

Reason 7. Take heed unto yourselves, for the honor of your Lord and Master and of his holy truth and ways lies more on you than on other men. As you may do him more service, so also you may do him more disservice than others. Would it not wound you to the heart to hear the name and truth of God reproached because of you? Would it not grieve you to see men point to you and say, "There goes a covetous priest, a secret drinker, a scandalous man. Here are those who preach for strictness when they themselves can live as loosely as others. They condemn us by their sermons and condemn themselves by their lives. For all their talk, they are as bad as we are." Brethren, could your heart endure to hear men cast the dung of your iniquities in the face of the holy God, of the gospel, and of all those who desire to fear the Lord? Would it not break your heart to think on it, that all the poor godly

Christians about you should suffer reproach for your misdoings? Oh, take heed in the name of God of every word that you speak and every step you tread, for you bear the ark of the Lord (Josh. 3:8, 17), you are entrusted with his honor, and dare you let it fall and cast it in the dirt?

Reason 8. Take heed unto yourselves, for the souls of your hearers and the success of all your labors very much depend on it. God prepares men for great works before he will make them his instruments in accomplishing them. He exercises men in those works to which they are most suited. If the work of the Lord is not soundly done upon your own hearts, how can you expect that he should bless your labors for the fulfilling of it in others? He may bless your labors if he chooses to, but you cannot be sure that he will.

Reasons Why Our Effectiveness Depends on Our Taking Heed

I here show you some further particular reasons under that last general reason.

First, can it be expected that God should bless that man's labors who works not for God but for himself? Such men make the ministry merely a trade to live by. They choose it rather than another calling because their parents directed them to it, because it is a life wherein they have more opportunity to furnish their intellects with all kinds of knowledge, because it is not so toilsome to the body for those who have a will to favor their flesh, because it is accompanied with some reverence and respect from men, because they think it a fine thing to be leaders and teachers and to have others depend on them and receive the law from their mouth (Mal. 2:7), and because it affords them a competent income. They are ministers for reasons such as these, and were it not for these ends, they would quickly cease being ministers. Can we expect God to bless the labors of men such as these? They preach not for him but for themselves and their own reputation or gain.

Second, how can you set yourselves day and night to a work that your carnal hearts are averse to? How can you call out with serious fervor to poor sinners to repent and come in to God when you never repented or came in yourselves? How can you heartily warn poor sinners with urgent appeals to take heed of sin and to set themselves to a holy life when you yourselves never felt the evil of sin or the worth of holiness? I tell you, these things are never well known until they are felt and never well felt until they are possessed. He who does not feel them himself is unlikely to speak feelingly to others or to help others to the feeling of them. How can you aid sinners with compassion in your hearts and tears in your eyes and beseech them in the name of the Lord to stop their course and return and live when you have never had so much compassion on your own souls as to do this much for yourselves?

Third, do you think it is a likely thing that he will fight against Satan with all his might who is a servant to Satan himself? Will he do any great harm to the kingdom of the devil who is himself a member and subject of that kingdom? Will he be true to Christ who is in covenant with his enemy, who does not have Christ in his heart? Why, this is the case of every unsanctified man, whatsoever cloth his coat is made of. Though many of these men may seem excellent preachers and cry down sin as loudly as others, yet it is all but an affected fervency and too often merely an ineffectual bawling. For he that cherishes sin in his own heart never falls upon it in others with godly sadness. An unsanctified man who loves the enemy is very unfit to be a leader in Christ's army. He who cleaves to the world and the flesh himself is unlikely to draw others to renounce them.

Fourth, it is unlikely that the people will value the doctrine of such men when they see that they do not live as they preach. They will think a man does not mean what he says if he does not live as he speaks. They will hardly believe a man who seems not to believe himself. If a man tells you to run for your life because a bear or an enemy is at your back, and yet he does not quicken his pace himself in the same way, you will be tempted to think that he is merely in jest and that there is really no such danger as he pretends. When preachers tell people that holiness is necessary and that without it no man will see the Lord (Heb. 12:14), and yet they remain unholy themselves, the people will think they preach only to pass away the hour because they must say something for their money. As long as men have eyes as well as ears, they will think they see your meaning as well as hear it, and they are more likely to believe their sight than their hearing.

All that a preacher says with his actions is a kind of preaching. When you live a covetous or careless life, you preach these sins to your people by your practice. Men will allow you to preach against their sins and encourage godliness as much as you like as long as you leave them alone afterward and be friendly and merry with them when you have finished. They will be content as long as you talk as they do and live as they do. For they take the pulpit to be just a stage where preachers must show themselves and play their parts, where you have liberty to say what you like for an hour. Is that man likely to do much good or be fit to be a minister of Christ who will speak for him an hour on Sunday and by his life will preach against him all the week besides?

Lastly, the success of your labors depends on the grace and blessing of the Lord, and where has he made any promise of his assistance and blessing to ungodly men? To his faithful servants he has promised that he will be with them (Matt. 28:20), that he will put his Spirit on them and his word in their mouths (Isa. 59:21), and that Satan will fall before them as lightning from heaven (Luke 10:17–18). But where is there any such promise to the ungodly, who are not the children of the promise? God may often do good to his church by wicked men but not so ordinarily nor to such a degree as by his own.

———

Questions for Reflection

1. Baxter begins a book on leadership with a clear-eyed look at leaders. Why do you think he starts there?

2. Baxter says that "you have a depraved nature and sinful inclinations as well as others do" (p. 36). Why is it so important to be aware of this? How do you see the truth of this assertion in yourself?

3. Reflect on Baxter's advice in this chapter. Which of his insights resonate with your experience? What other thoughts or advice would you add?

4. In this opening chapter, Baxter has set the tone for the whole book. What do you make of that tone? How is it sitting with you?

5. As you look around, you will see examples of pastors whose public sin has discredited their ministry. How will you put Baxter's advice into practice so that you finish well in your own ministry?

Take Heed unto All the Flock

Having laid out the responsibility of pastors to pay close attention to themselves, Baxter now turns to the second half of Paul's instruction: "Take heed unto . . . all the flock." His starting proposition is that congregations should not be so large that the pastor or pastors in that church are unable to know their members individually. He then moves on to consider what pastors are to teach church members and the different kinds of people they are likely to encounter. Such people range from those who are still in need of conversion to those who are strong, established believers. Finally, Baxter identifies ten different aspects of each minister's work.

———

HAVING SHOWED YOU WHAT IT IS to take heed unto ourselves and why it must be done, I will next show you what it is to take heed unto all the flock. But before we speak of the work itself, we must begin with what is implied and presupposed.

The Appropriate Size of a Church

First, it is here implied that every flock should have its own pastor (one or more) and every pastor his own flock. As every troop or company in a regiment of soldiers must have its own captain and other officers, and every soldier know his own commanders, so it is the will of God that all churches should have their own pastors and that all Christ's disciples should know their teachers who are over them in the Lord (1 Thess. 5:12–13). The universal church of Christ must consist of individual churches guided by their own overseers, and every Christian must be a member of one of these churches (except those who are away on business or travel or are in other similar cases of necessity). Though a minister is an officer in the universal church, yet in a special manner he is the overseer of that particular church committed to his charge.

Second, when we are commanded to take heed unto all the flock, it is plainly implied that our flock must be ordinarily no greater than we are capable of overseeing or taking heed of. For God will not lay on us natural impossibilities. He will not require men to leap up to the moon, to touch the stars, or to number the sands of the sea. If it is the pastoral work to oversee and take heed unto all the flock, then surely there must be such a proportion of pastors assigned to each flock or such a number of souls in the care of each pastor that he is able to take such heed unto his people as is here required. Oh, happy church of Christ, where the laborers are able and faithful and so proportioned to the number of souls that they might be able to take heed unto all their flock.

Taking Care of All the Flock

Having told you these two things that are here implied, I now come to the duty itself. Taking heed unto all the flock in general requires very great care of every person with great watchfulness and diligence. It calls on the use of all those holy actions and ordinances that God has required us to use for their salvation.

The subject matter of the ministerial work is in general spiritual things or matters that concern the pleasing of God and the salvation of our people. It is the first and greatest work of the ministers of Christ to acquaint men with the God who made them and is their happiness, to open to them the treasures of his goodness, and to tell them of the glory that is in his presence, which all his chosen people will enjoy. By showing men the certainty and excellency of the promised felicity and perfect blessedness of the life to come compared with the vanities of this present life, we may turn the stream of their thoughts and affections, bring them to a due contempt of this world, and set them on seeking the durable treasure (Matt. 6:19–20).

Then we have the great mystery of redemption to disclose: the person, incarnation, perfection, life, miracles, sufferings, death, burial, resurrection, ascension, glorification, dominion, and intercession of the blessed Son of God. Oh, what a treasury of his blessings, his inner workings of grace in our lives, and the privileges of his saints we have to unfold! What a blessed life of holiness and communion we have to recommend to the sons of men. Yet how many temptations, difficulties, and dangers we have to disclose and assist them against! How many precious spiritual duties we have to set them upon, and excite them to, and direct them in! How many objections of flesh and blood, and frivolous objections of vain men, we have to confute! How much of their own corruptions and sinful inclinations we have to discover and root out! We have the depth of God's bottomless love and mercy to disclose; the depth of the mysteries of his designs and works of creation, redemption, providence, justification, adoption, sanctification, and glorification; the depth of Satan's temptations; and the depth of their own hearts.

In a word, we must teach our people as much as we can of the whole word and works of God. All Christians are students of Christ: the church is his school, he is the head teacher, we are his underteachers, the Bible is his book of grammar, and all this is what we must be teaching them daily.

The object of our pastoral care is all the flock, that is, the church and every member of it. We should know every person who belongs to our charge. For how can we take heed unto them if we do not know them? A careful shepherd looks after every individual sheep. A good schoolmaster looks to every individual student, both for instruction and correction. A good physician looks after every particular patient. And good commanders look after every individual soldier. Why, then, should the teachers, the pastors, the physicians, the guides of the churches of Christ not take heed unto every individual member of their charge?

Christ himself is the great and good shepherd and master of the church, who has the whole church to look after and yet takes care of every individual in it. In Luke 15, he tells us that he is like the shepherd who leaves the ninety-nine sheep in the wilderness to seek out the one that was lost; or like the woman who lights a candle, sweeps the house, and searches diligently to find the one coin that was lost, and having found it, she rejoices and calls her friends and neighbors to rejoice with her. Christ tells us that there is joy in heaven over one sinner who repents (Luke 15:7, 10). The prophets were often sent to single men. Ezekiel was made a watchman over individuals who must say to the wicked, "You shall surely die" (Ezek. 3:18–19). Paul taught the people publicly and from house to house (Acts 20:20), which refers to his teaching particular families. The same Paul warned every man and taught every man, in all wisdom, that he might present every man perfect in Christ Jesus (Col. 1:28). Christ explained his public parables to the twelve on their own (Mark 4:34). Every man must seek the law at the mouth of the priest (Mal. 2:7). As pastors, we must give an account of our watching over the souls of all who are bound to obey us (Heb. 13:17). Many more passages in Scripture assure us that it is our duty to take heed unto every individual person in our flock.

You might object that the congregation you are set over is so large that it is not possible for you to know all the people, much less to take heed of them individually. I answer, were you forced to take on such a charge, or did you choose? If you chose, you excuse one sin with another. How dare you undertake that which you knew yourself to be unable to perform when you were not forced to it? It seems, then, that you had some other ends in your undertaking and never intended to make it good and be faithful to your trust.

But if you think that you were compelled to undertake so great a charge, I must ask you, could you not have sought assistance? Have you done all that you could with your friends and neighbors to get income for another to help you? Do you not have so much income that it could serve yourself and an assistant even though that will not serve to maintain you in fullness? Is it not better to constrain your flesh and your family than to undertake a work that you cannot do and thus neglect the souls of so many men?

I know this will seem hard to some, but to me it seems an unquestionable thing that if you have a comfortable income, it is your duty to live on part of it and give the rest to a competent assistant rather than allow the flock that you are over to be neglected. You might say, "This is a hard measure; my wife and children cannot live like that." I answer, do not many families in your parish live on less? Can your parishioners better endure damnation than you can endure lack and poverty? You call yourselves ministers of the gospel; are the souls of men so worthless in your eyes that you would rather they eternally perished than that you and your family should live in a low and poor condition?

I must further say that this poverty is not so sad and dangerous a business as it is pretended to be. If you have basic food and clothing, should you not be content with that? Would you have more than you need for the work of God? It is not purple and fine linen or faring deliciously every day (Luke 16:19) that you should look for. A man's life does not consist in the abundance of the things that he possesses (Luke 12:15). As long as your clothing is warm and your food is wholesome, you may as well be supported by it to serve God as if you had the fullest satisfaction to your flesh. A patched coat may still be warm; bread and drink is wholesome food. He who has these has a cold excuse for hazarding men's souls so that he may live on a fuller diet in the world.

Recognizing the Differences among the Flock

We are next to consider the work in reference to the different kinds of members in our churches. The first part of our ministerial work lies in bringing unsound professors of the faith to sincerity, so that those who are Christians only in name and show may be Christians indeed. We have, therefore, a work of great necessity to do for them, even to open their eyes and turn them from darkness to light and from the power of Satan to God, so that they may receive forgiveness of sins and an inheritance among the sanctified by faith in Christ (Acts 26:18). We work to soften and open their hearts to the reception of the truth, if God perhaps will give them the repentance necessary to acknowledge it, so that those souls may escape the snare of the devil who have been taken captive by him at his will (2 Tim. 2:25–26). We work so they may be converted and their sins may be forgiven (Mark 4:12).

As Paul's spirit was stirred within him when he saw the Athenians so addicted to idolatry (Acts 17:16–17), so it should call us to a similar urgency to see so many men in great probability of being everlastingly undone. If by faith we did indeed look on them as within a step of hell, it should more effectually untie our tongues. The man who will let a sinner go to hell for lack of speaking to him sets less by souls than the Redeemer of souls did and less by his neighbor than rational charity will allow him to do by his greatest enemy. Oh, brethren, whomsoever you neglect, neglect not the most miserable! Whatever you pass over, forget not poor souls who are under the condemnation and curse of the law and may expect at any hour the infernal execution of that curse if a speedy change does not prevent it. Oh, call after the impenitent and advance this great work of converting souls whatever else you leave undone.

The next part of the ministerial work is for the building up of those who are already truly converted. According to the various states of these converts, the work is various. First, many of our flock are young and weak. Though of long standing, they are yet of small proficiency or strength (Heb. 5:11–13). Indeed, it is the most common condition of the godly: most of them remain in weak and low degrees of grace, and it is no easy matter to get them higher. It is a very troublesome thing to be weak. It keeps us under dangers. It abates our consolation and delight in God, and it takes off the sweetness of his ways. It makes us go about our work with too much backwardness and come away with little peace or profit. It makes us less serviceable to God and man, brings less honor to our Master and profession, and does less good to all those about us. We find small benefit by the means we use. We too easily play with the serpent's baits and are ensnared by his wiles. We are less able to resist and stand in an encounter (Eph. 6:11, 13). We fall sooner, and it is harder to rise.

Seeing that the case of the weak is comparatively so sad, how diligent should we be to cherish and increase their grace! The strength of Christians is the honor of the church. Oh, what an honor it is when men are inflamed with the love of God, live by a lively, working faith, set little store on the profits and honors of the world, love one another fervently with a pure heart (1 Pet. 1:22), can bear and heartily forgive a wrong (Col. 3:13), suffer joyfully for the cause of Christ, study to do good, and walk inoffensively and harmlessly in the world. They are ready to be servants of all men for their good, becoming all things to all men to win them (1 Cor. 9:22) and yet abstaining from the appearances of evil (1 Thess. 5:22) and seasoning all their actions with a sweet mixture of prudence, humility, zeal, and heavenly spirituality. It is, therefore, a necessary part of our work to labor more in the polishing and perfecting of the saints so that they may be strong in the Lord (Eph. 6:10) and fitted for their Master's use (2 Tim. 2:21).

A second group of converts who need our special help are those who labor under some particular distemper that inhibits the inner workings of God's grace and makes them temptations and troubles to others and a burden to themselves. For alas, there are too many like this: some who are especially addicted to pride, some to worldliness, some to this or that sensual desire, and many to perversity and disturbing passions. It is our duty to work for the assistance of all these, partly by dissuasions and clear discoveries of the odiousness of their sin and partly by suitable directions to help them to a fuller conquest of their corruptions. We must be no more gentle on the sins of the godly than on those of the ungodly. Ministers of Christ must do their duty and must not so far hate their brother as to forbear the plain rebuking of him or suffer sin to lie on his soul (Lev. 19:17). Though it must be done with much prudence, yet done it must be.

A third sort are declining Christians who have either fallen into some scandalous sin or have abated their zeal and diligence and thus show us that they have lost their former love (Rev. 2:4). As the case of backsliders is very sad, so our diligence must be great for their recovery.

A fourth part of the ministerial work is with those who have fallen under some great temptation. Much of our assistance is necessary to our people in such a case. Therefore, every minister should be a man who has much insight into the tempter's wiles. We should know the great variety of them, the cunning craft of all Satan's instruments that lie in wait to deceive (Eph. 4:14), and the methods and devices of the grand deceiver.

Some of our people lie under temptations to error and heresy. Others lie under a temptation to worldliness, others to gluttony or drunkenness, others to lust, some to one sin, and some to another. A faithful pastor, therefore, should have his eye on them all and labor to be acquainted with their natural temperament, with their occasions and affairs in the world, and with the company that they live or converse with. Knowing where their temptations lie, he can then speedily, prudently, and diligently seek to help them.

A fifth part of our work is to comfort the disconsolate and to settle the peace of our people's souls on sure and lasting grounds. To that end, the quality of the individual complainants and the course of their lives needs to be known, for all people must not have the same consolations who have similar complaints.

The rest of our ministerial work is on those who are strong, for they also have need of our assistance. This is partly to prevent their temptations and declinings and to preserve the grace they have, partly to help them for a further progress and increase, and partly to direct them in the improving of their strength for the service of Christ and the assistance of their brethren. We are also to encourage them—especially the aged, the tempted, and the afflicted—to persevere so that they may attain the crown of life (Rev. 2:10).

All these are the objects of the ministerial work, and in respect to all these we must take heed unto all the flock.

Putting This into Practice

Having discussed our work in respect of its objects, I will next speak of the acts themselves. Here I will be very brief because these acts are intimated before, they are so fully handled by many, and I find I have already run into more tediousness than I intended.

One part of our work, the most excellent part because it tends to work on many, is the public preaching of the word. This is a work that requires greater skill and especially greater life and zeal than any of us brings to it. It is no small matter to stand up in the face of a congregation and deliver a message of salvation or damnation as from the living God in the name of our Redeemer. It is no easy matter to speak so plainly that the ignorant may understand us, so seriously that the deadest hearts may feel us, and so convincingly that the contradicting objectors may be silenced.

Another part of our pastoral work is to administer the holy mysteries, or seals, of God's covenant: baptism and the Lord's Supper. Another part of our work is to guide our people and be their mouth in the public prayers of the church and the public praises of God and to bless them in the name of the Lord. This part of the work is not the least, nor is it to be so much thrust into a corner as it is by too many of us.

Another part of the ministerial work is to have a special care and oversight of each member of the flock. This entails the following requirements:

1. We must labor to be acquainted with the state of all our people as fully as we can, to know both the individuals and their inclinations and way of living. Thus we will know what sins they are most in danger of, what duties they neglect, and what temptations they are most liable to. For if we do not know the temperament or disease, we are likely to prove unsuccessful physicians.

2. We must use all the means we can to instruct the ignorant in the matters of their salvation. We must do this by our own most plain, familiar words; by giving or lending them books that are fit for them; by persuading them to learn catechisms (and those who cannot read, to get help from their neighbors); and by persuading their neighbors, who have the best opportunities, to afford them help.

3. We must be ready to give advice to those who come to us with cases of conscience, especially the great case that the Jews put to Peter (Acts 2:37) and the jailer to Paul and Silas (Acts 16:30): "What must we do to be saved?" A minister is not only to be about public preaching but also to be a known counselor for his people's souls, as the lawyer is for their estates and the physician is for their bodies, so that each man who is in doubts and difficulties should bring his case to the minister and desire resolution. Not that a minister should be troubled with every small matter that judicious neighbors can help with as well as he, no more than a lawyer or physician should be troubled for every trifling or familiar case in which others can tell them as much as a lawyer or physician can. But just as when their

estate or life is in danger they will go to their lawyer or physician, so when their souls are in danger they should go to their minister. This is how Nicodemus came to Christ (John 3:1–2) and how the people of Israel went to the priest, whose lips must preserve knowledge and from whose mouth they must ask the law, because he is the messenger of the Lord of hosts (Mal. 2:7).

Because the people have grown unacquainted with the office of the ministry and with their own necessity and duty, it belongs to us to acquaint them with this office and to press them publicly to come to us for advice in cases of great concern to their souls. We must not only be willing to undertake the trouble but also be willing to draw it upon ourselves by inviting them to come to us. How few have I ever heard who heartily pressed their people to their duty in this regard? It is a sad case that people's souls should be so injured and hazarded by the total neglect of so great a duty, and yet ministers scarcely ever tell them of it and awaken them to it! If your people were duly sensible of the need and weight of this duty, you would have them more frequently knocking at your door to open their lives to you, make their sad complaints, and beg your advice. I beseech you to urge them more on this duty in the future and perform it carefully when they seek your help. To this end, it is very necessary that we are acquainted with practical cases, and especially that we are acquainted with the nature of true grace and resolve the main question that concerns people's everlasting life or death. One word of seasonable, prudent advice given by a minister to an individual in need has done more good than many sermons would have done.

4. We must also have a special eye on families to see that they are well ordered and that the duties of each member are performed. The life of religion and the welfare and glory of church and state depend

much on family government and duty. If we suffer the neglect of this matter, we undo all. What are we likely to achieve for the reforming of our congregation if all the work is cast on us alone, and if masters of families neglect that necessary duty of their own by which they are bound to help us? If our work begins to do some good in any of our people, a careless, prayerless, worldly family is likely to stifle it or very much hinder it. But if you could get the rulers of families to do their part and take up the work where you left it and help it along, what abundance of good might be done by it? I beseech you, therefore, do all that you can to promote this business if ever you desire the true reformation and welfare of your parishes. You are likely to see no general reformation until you procure family reformation.

5. Another part of the work of our private oversight consists in a vigilant opposing of those who work to seduce weak Christians with false doctrine. We must seek to prevent the infection of our flock and speedily reclaim those who begin to itch after strange teachers and turn into crooked paths (Isa. 59:8). When we hear of anyone who lies under the influence of these temptations or who is already deceived by them, we must speedily and with all our skill and diligence attend to their relief.

6. Another part of this oversight lies in the due encouragement of those who are humble, upright, obedient Christians, who profit by our teaching and are an honor to their profession of faith. We must in the eyes of all the flock distinguish them from the rest by our praises, our more special familiarity, and other testimonies of our approval and rejoicing over them. This will both encourage them and provoke others to imitate them.

7. Another part of our oversight lies in visiting the sick and helping them prepare either for a fruitful life or a happy death. Though

this is the main business of all our life and theirs, yet at such a season it requires extraordinary care of both them and us. When time is almost gone and they must be now or never reconciled to God and possessed of his grace, oh, how does it concern them to redeem those hours and lay hold of eternal life! When we see that we are likely to have but a few days' or hours' more time to speak to them about their endless state, what man who is not an infidel or an unfeeling block would not be with them and do all that he can for their salvation in that short space?

Will it not awaken us to compassion to look on a languishing man and to think that within a few days his soul will be in heaven or hell? Surely it will test the faith and seriousness of ministers to be with dying men: they will have much opportunity to discern whether they are themselves in good earnest about the matters of the life to come. So great is the change made by death that it should awaken us to the greatest sensibility to see a man so near it and should provoke in us the deepest pangs of compassion.

8. Another part of our ministerial oversight consists in comforting the consciences of the troubled and in settling our people in a well-grounded peace.

9. Another part of this oversight is in reproving and admonishing those who live offensively or impenitently, and receiving the information of those who have admonished them more privately in vain. Before we bring such matters to the church (Matt. 18:17), it is ordinarily most fit for the minister to see what he can do more privately to bring the sinner to repentance, especially if it is not a public crime. A great deal of skill is here required, and we must distinguish according to the various tempers of the offenders. But with most it will be necessary to pursue the work with the greatest plainness and power to

shake their careless hearts and make them see what it is to dally with sin. Let them know the evil of it and its sad effects, the unkindness, unreasonableness, unprofitableness, and other aggravations of sin, and what it is that they do against God and themselves.

10. The final part of our oversight lies in the use of church discipline. This consists in more public reproof, in persuading the offender to appropriate expressions of repentance, in praying for them, in restoring the penitent, and in excluding and avoiding the impenitent (Matt. 18:15–17).

Many men assume that the pastoral office consists only in preaching and administering the sacraments. From what has been said, we may see that it is another kind of thing—and so much more than they think.

Questions for Reflection

1. Baxter says that "we should know every person who belongs to our charge. For how can we take heed unto them if we do not know them?" (p. 48). Do you agree?

2. Is Baxter correct when he says that churches should not be so large that the pastor (or pastors) cannot know each believer individually?

3. Think about your church. If you are a pastor, do you know each person individually?

4. Baxter is driven by the urgency of diligently and intentionally providing for the soul life of each member of his congregation. Do you share his urgency? Is his instinct correct, or is he being too demanding?

5. As you look back over this chapter, which of Baxter's suggestions, assumptions, or challenges surprise you?

6. In what practical ways might Baxter's prescription change the way you pay close attention to all the flock?

The Ministerial Work

All pastors have vital work to do in keeping watch over all the flock, but how are they to carry themselves in that work? This is Baxter's next question, to which he offers fourteen answers. Taken together, they explain the manner in which pastors are to fulfill their responsibilities and duties across the full range of their ministry.

———

HAVING SPOKEN OF THE MATTER of our work, we are next to speak a little of the manner, addressing the whole course of our ministry in general.

The Shape of Our Work

1. The ministerial work must be managed purely for God and the salvation of the people and not for any private ends of our own. This is our sincerity in it. A wrong end makes all the work bad, no matter how good in itself. It is serving not God but ourselves if we do it not for God but for ourselves. Self-denial is of absolute necessity in every Christian, but it is of a double necessity in a minister, as he has a double sanctification or dedication to God. Without self-denial, he cannot

do God an hour's faithful service. Hard studies, much knowledge, and excellent preaching are but a more glorious hypocritical sinning if the ends are not right.

2. This work must be managed laboriously and diligently, as being of such unspeakable consequence to others and ourselves. We are seeking to uphold the world, to save it from the curse of God, to perfect the creation, to attain the ends of Christ's redemption, to save ourselves and others from damnation, to overcome the devil and demolish his kingdom, to set up the kingdom of Christ, and to attain and help others attain the kingdom of glory. Are these works to be done with a careless mind or a lazy hand? Oh, see that this work is done with all your might (Eccles. 9:10). Study hard, for the well is deep, and our brains are shallow. Especially be laborious in the practice and exercise of your knowledge. Let Paul's words ring in your ears continually: "Necessity is laid on me, and woe unto me if I do not preach the gospel" (1 Cor. 9:16). Think to yourself what lies on your hands: "If I do not stir myself, Satan may prevail, and my people may everlastingly perish, and their blood will be required at my hand (Ezek. 3:18). By avoiding labor and suffering, I will draw upon me a thousand times more labor and suffering than I avoid."

3. This work must be carried on prudently, orderly, and by degrees. Milk must go before strong food. The foundation must first be laid before we build on it. Children must not be dealt with as grown men. Men must be brought into a state of grace before we can expect from them the works of grace. The work of conversion, repentance from dead works, and faith in Christ (Heb. 6:1) must be first and frequently and thoroughly taught. The stewards of God's household must give to each servant his portion in due season (Luke 12:42). We must ordinarily not go beyond the capacities of

our people, nor teach them the perfection if they have not learned the principles.

4. Through the whole course of our ministry, we must insist most on the greatest, most certain, and necessary things, and be more seldom and sparing on the rest. If we teach Christ to our people, we teach them all. Get them well to heaven, and they will have knowledge enough. The great and commonly acknowledged truths are those that men must live on. They are the great instruments of raising the heart to God and of destroying men's sins. Other things are desirable to be known, but these must be known, or else our people are undone forever.

I think necessity should be a great disposer of a minister's course of study and labors. If we were sufficient for everything, we might absorb everything and work through the whole encyclopedia. But life is short and we are dull, eternal things are necessary, and the souls that depend on our teaching are precious. I confess that necessity has been the conductor of my studies and life. It chooses what book I will read and tells me when and for how long. It chooses my text and gives my sermon both matter and manner, so far as I can keep out my own corruption. Though I know my constant expectation of death has been a great cause of this, yet I know no reason why the most healthy man should not make sure of the necessaries first, considering the uncertainty and shortness of all men's lives. Hence it is that a preacher must often return to the same things, because the matters of necessity are few.

5. All our teaching must be as plain and evident as we can make it, for this most suits a teacher's ends. He who seeks to be understood must speak to the capacity of his hearers and make it his business to make himself understood. Truth loves the light and is most beautiful

when it is most naked. If you would not teach men, why are you in the pulpit? If you would teach men, why do you not speak so as to be understood?

The Character We Must Bring to Our Work

1. Our whole work must be carried on in a sense of our insufficiency and in a pious, believing dependence on Christ. We must go to him for light, life, and strength who sends us to work. When our own faith is weak, when our hearts grow dull and unsuitable to so great a work as ours, we must have recourse to the Lord who sends us. Prayer as well as preaching must carry on our work. He who will not pray for his people cannot preach heartily to his people. If we do not prevail with God to give the people faith and repentance, we are unlikely to prevail with them to believe and repent. Paul gives us his example of praying night and day for his hearers (1 Thess. 3:10). When our own hearts are so far out of order, and theirs so far out of order, if we do not prevail with God to mend and help them, we are likely to make our work unsuccessful.

2. Our work must be managed with great humility. We must carry ourselves meekly and humbly to all. We must teach others as men who are ready to learn from anyone who can teach us, and so both teach and learn at once.

3. There must be a prudent mixture of severity and mildness both in our preaching and church discipline. Each must be predominant according to the quality of the person or matter that we have in hand. If there is no severity, there will be contempt for our reproofs. If there is only severity, we will be taken as usurpers of dominion rather than persuaders of the minds of men to the truth.

4. We must be sincerely affectionate, serious, and zealous in all our public and private exhortations. The weight of our matter con-

demns coldness and sleepy dullness. We should ensure that we are well awakened ourselves and our spirits in such a state as may make us fit to awaken others. If our words are not sharpened and do not pierce as nails, they will hardly be felt by stony hearts. To speak coldly and slightly of heavenly things is nearly as bad as to say nothing of them.

5. All our work must be managed reverently, as is fitting for those who believe in the presence of God and do not use holy things as if they were common (Ezek. 22:26). The more of God that appears in our duties, the more authority they will have with men. Reverence is that affection of the soul that proceeds from deep apprehensions of God and signifies a mind that is much conversant with him. To show irreverence in the things of God is to show hypocrisy and that the heart agrees not with the tongue. I cannot speak for others, but the most reverent preacher who speaks as if he saw the face of God has more effect on my heart, though with common words, than an irreverent man has even with the most exquisite preparations. He may bawl it out with what looks like genuine earnestness, but fervency that is not balanced with reverence achieves little. Of all preaching in the world (that does not speak lies), I hate that preaching that tends to make the hearers laugh or to move their minds with tickling levity and affect them as stage plays do, instead of affecting them with a holy reverence for the name of God. We should imagine that we saw the throne of God and the millions of glorious angels attending him so that we might be awed with his majesty when we draw near him in his holy things, lest we profane them and take his name in vain (Ex. 20:7).

6. All our work must be done spiritually as by men possessed by the Holy Spirit and led by him and as men who savor the things of the Spirit. There is in some men's preaching a spiritual strain that spiritual hearers can discern and relish. But in some men's

preaching, this sacred tincture is so lacking that even when they speak of spiritual things, it is as if they spoke of common matters. Our evidence must be spiritual, drawn from Holy Scripture. Esteem the church fathers and other writers, but value none of them as equivalent to the word of God. We will not refuse their service, but we must abhor them as competitors. It is a sign of a distempered heart that loses the relish of Scripture's excellence.

7. The whole course of our ministry must be carried on in a tender love to our people. We must let them see that nothing pleases us but what profits them, that what does them good does us good, and that nothing troubles us more than their hurt. We must remember that pastors are not lords but fathers and therefore must be affectionate to their people as to their own children. The tenderest love of a mother should not surpass theirs. We must travail in giving birth to them until Christ is formed in them (Gal. 4:19). They should see that we care for no outward thing, not money, not liberty, not credit, not life, in comparison with their salvation. Thus we should, as John says, be ready "to lay down our lives for the brethren" (1 John 3:16), and with Paul not to count our lives dear to us, so that we may finish our course with joy in doing the work of God for their salvation (Acts 20:24). When the people see that you genuinely love them, they will hear anything and bear anything and will follow you more easily. We ourselves will take all things well from one who we know loves us entirely. Therefore, see that you feel a tender love for your people, and then let them feel it in your speeches and see it in your dealings. Let them see that you spend and are spent for their sakes (2 Cor. 12:15) and that all you do is for them and not for any ends of your own. To this end, the works of charity are necessary as far as your capacities will reach, for bare words will hardly convince men that you have any great love for them.

8. Another necessary quality of our work is patience. We must bear with many abuses and injuries from those for whom we are doing good. We have studied for them and prayed for them. We have beseeched and exhorted them with all humility. We have spent ourselves for them and given them what we are able. We have nurtured them as if they had been our children. Yet we must expect that many will repay us with scorn, hatred, and contempt. Expect them to cast our kindness back in our faces with disdain and take us for their enemies because we tell them the truth (Gal. 4:16). The more we love, the less we will be loved (2 Cor. 12:15). All this must be patiently undergone, and still we must unweariedly hold on in doing good (Gal. 6:9). We have to deal with distracted men who will fly in the face of their physician, but we must not therefore forsake their cure.

9. Let me conclude with one thing necessary to us as fellow laborers in the work. We must be very studious of union and communion among ourselves and of the unity and peace of the churches that we oversee. We must be aware how necessary this is to the prosperity of the whole church, the strengthening of our common cause, the good of the individual members of our flock, and the further enlargement of the kingdom of Christ. Therefore, ministers must feel the pain when the church is wounded and be so far from being the leaders in divisions that they should take it as a principal part of their work to prevent and heal them.

Questions for Reflection

1. How would you summarize Baxter's vision of an ideal pastor, that is, a reformed pastor?

2. What values are revealed in Baxter's directions? In what ways do you share those values and reflect them in your own ministry? In what ways do you need to change and grow?

3. This chapter has been about "the whole course of our ministry in general" (p. 61). How does Baxter balance the various dimensions of ministry? What part does our character play in our ministry?

4. "A wrong end makes all the work bad, no matter how good in itself" (p. 61). What are your motivations for ministry? How do you weigh up your wants and needs against the needs and demands of ministry?

5. At this point in the book, how is Baxter's sheer earnestness and urgency sitting with you? What emotional reactions do you notice when you read his words? Do you feel uncomfortable, guilty, inspired, energized, awkward, condemned, or alienated by Baxter's thoughts and words? How are you responding to any feelings of discouragement or inadequacy?

What a Subtle Enemy Is
This Sin of Pride!

When Baxter planned to gather with his fellow ministers in December 1655, it was for "the solemn humbling of their souls before the Lord" because they had neglected for so long the work of regular, personal, private instruction of families: "And how should we be humbled without a plain confession of our sin?"[1] Yet Baxter does not begin The Reformed Pastor *with this "plain confession." He brings it in only now, in the fourth chapter. It is likely that after his exposition in the first three chapters, his audience was acutely aware of the ways in which they had fallen short of Baxter's ideal. This is, then, an appropriate moment for confession and repentance, beginning with the fundamental sin of pride.*

———

OUR BUSINESS IS TO HUMBLE our souls before the Lord for our former negligence, especially our negligence of catechizing and personally instructing those committed to our charge, and to desire God's assistance in our undertaken employment for the time to come.

---

1   Richard Baxter, *The Reformed Pastor* (London, 1656), preface, sig. A2v, A3r.

Indeed, we can scarcely expect the latter without the former. If God will help us in our future duty and amendment, he will surely humble us first for our former sin. Change cannot go without some good measure of sorrow. Indeed, we may justly here begin our confessions: it is too common with us to expect from our people that of which we do little or nothing ourselves. What pains we take to humble them, while we ourselves are unhumbled! If only we studied half as much to affect and amend our own hearts as we do our hearers' hearts, it would not be with many of us as it is.

Confessing Our Sins

We find that the guides of the church in Scripture confessed in tears their own sins as well as the sins of the people. Ezra confessed the sins of the priests as well as those of the people, weeping and casting himself down before the house of God (Ezra 9:6–7, 10; 10:1). So did the Levites (Neh. 9:32–35). Daniel confessed his own sin as well as the people's (Dan. 9:20), and God calls others to it (Joel 2:15–17). When the fast is summoned, the people gathered, the congregation sanctified, and the elders assembled, the priests and ministers of the Lord are called to begin with weeping and crying out to God for mercy (Joel 1:13–14).

I think if we well consider the duties already examined, we have no need to question whether we have reason for the same sort of humiliation. I must say, though I judge myself in saying it, that he who reads even this one exhortation of Paul in Acts 20:28 and compares his life with it is too stupid and hard-hearted if he does not melt in the sense of his neglect and fly for refuge to the blood of Christ and to his pardoning grace. It is a sad thing that so many of us preach our hearers asleep, but it is sadder still if we have studied and preached ourselves asleep and have talked so long against hardness of heart until our own hearts grow hardened under the noise of our own reproofs.

So that you may see that God calls us not to a causeless sorrow, I will take it to be my duty to call to remembrance our many sins, or those that are most obvious. I will set them this day before God and our own faces, that God may cast them behind his back (Isa. 38:17). I will deal plainly and faithfully in a free confession so that he who is faithful and just may forgive them (1 John 1:9). I will judge ourselves so that we will not be judged by the Lord (1 Cor. 11:31). I will suppose I have your free and hearty consent and that, far from being offended with the disgrace, you will readily accept the charge and be humble self-accusers.

So far am I from justifying myself by accusing others that I sincerely put my name with the first in the list of accused. For how can a wretched sinner of so great transgressions presume to justify himself with God? How can he plead guiltless whose conscience has so much to say against him? If I cast shame on the ministry, it is not on the office but on our persons by opening that sin that is our shame. For sin is a reproach to any people (Prov. 14:34), and it is myself as well as others on whom I must lay the shame.

Only I must first say this: for all the faults that are now among us, I do not believe that England ever had such an able and faithful ministry as it has at this day, and I fear that few nations on earth, if any, have the like. I bless the Lord that he has placed me in such a neighborhood where I may have the brotherly fellowship of so many able, humble, peaceable, and faithful men. Oh, that the Lord would long continue this admirable mercy. All this is the due acknowledgment of God's gracious provision so that I may not seem unthankful in confession, much less to cloud or vilify God's provision while I open the frailties that accompany them in many ministers.

The Particular Sin of Pride

One of our most heinous and palpable sins is pride, a sin that has too much interest in the best but is more hateful and inexcusable in us than in other men. Pride fills some minister's minds with aspiring desires and designs. It possesses them with envious and bitter thoughts against those who stand in their light, eclipse their glory, or hinder the progress of their idolized reputation. Oh, what a constant companion, what a tyrannous commander, what a sly and subtle insinuating enemy is this sin of pride! It goes with men to the draper, the mercer, the tailor, where it chooses their cloth, their trimming, and their fashion. It dresses them in the morning, at least on the outside. Fewer ministers would follow the fashion in hair and clothing if it were not for the command of this tyrannical vice.

If only that were all, or the worst, but alas, how frequently does pride come with us into our studies and sit with us as we prepare our sermon? How often does it choose our subject and more often choose our words and ornaments? God bids us to be as plain as we can for the informing of the ignorant and as convincing and serious as we are able for the melting and changing of unchanged hearts. But pride stands by and contradicts all. Sometimes it puts in toys and trifles. It pollutes rather than polishes, and under pretense of laudable ornaments, it dishonors our sermons with childish toys. It persuades us to paint the window that it may dim the light and to speak to our people that which they cannot understand. Then when pride has made our sermon, it goes with us into the pulpit. It forms our tone and animates our delivery. It causes us to avoid that which may be displeasing to our hearers, however necessary, and sets us in a pursuit of vain applause.

The sum of all this is that pride makes men both in studying and preaching to seek themselves and deny God, when they should seek God's glory and deny themselves. If they perceive that they are highly thought of, they rejoice that they have attained their end. But if they perceive that they are thought weak or common men, they are displeased at having missed the prize of the day.

Yet even this is not all, nor the worst. Oh, that ever it should be spoken of godly ministers that they are so set on popular approval and of sitting highest in men's estimation that they envy the gifts and names of their brethren who are preferred before them. They act as if all were taken from their praises that is given to another's. They carry themselves as if God had given them his gifts so that they may walk as men of reputation in the world, and all his gifts in others are to be trodden down and vilified if they seem to stand in the way of their honor! Will a saint, a preacher for Christ, envy that which has the image of Christ and malign his gifts for which he should have the glory, all because those gifts in others seem to hinder his own glory? Every true Christian is a member of the body and therefore shares in the blessings of the whole body and of each particular member. Every man owes thanks to God for his brother's gifts, just as the foot benefits from the guidance of the eye and also because his own ends may be attained by his brother's gifts as well as by his own (1 Cor. 12:12–27). If the glory of God and the church's felicity are not his end, he is not a Christian. Will any workman malign another because he helps him do his Master's work? Yet alas, how common is this heinous crime among men of leadership and eminency in the church!

Thus it is that men magnify their own opinions and criticize anyone who differs from them in lesser matters, as if it were all the same thing to differ from them and from God. They expect that all men should be conformed to their judgments as if they were the rule of the church's faith! It is true, we have more modesty than expressly to say so. We pretend that we expect men should yield only to the evidence of truth that appears in our reasons and that our zeal is for the truth and not for ourselves. But as that must be taken for truth that is ours, so our reasons must be taken as valid. We embrace the cause of our errors as if all that was said against them was spoken against our persons and as if we were heinously injured to have our arguments thoroughly confuted by which we ourselves injured the truth and the minds of men!

So high are our spirits that when it becomes a duty to any man to reprove or contradict us, we are commonly impatient both of the matter and of the manner. We love the man who will say as we say, be of our opinion, and promote our reputation, though he be less worthy of our love in other respects. But he is displeasing to us who contradicts us and differs from us, who deals plainly with us in our miscarriages, and who tells us of our faults. Our pride makes too many of us think all men hate us who do not admire us and admire all that we say and who do not submit their judgments to our most palpable mistakes! We are so tender that no man can scarce touch us but we are hurt. We are so stout and high-minded that a man can hardly speak to us.

I confess that I have often marveled that this most heinous sin should be thought so consistent with a holy frame of heart and life when far lesser sins are by ourselves proclaimed to be so damnable in our people! I have been amazed to see the difference between ungodly sinners and godly preachers in this respect. When we speak to drunkards, worldlings, or any ignorant, unconverted men, we disgrace them as in that condition to the utmost. We lay it on as plainly as we can speak and tell them of their sin, shame, and misery. We expect that they should not only bear all this patiently but also take all this thankfully. Most of those I deal with do take it patiently, and many gross sinners will most commend the starkest preachers. They will say that they care not to hear a man who will not tell them plainly of their sins. But if we speak to godly ministers against their errors or any sin, even though we honor them, reverence them, and speak as smoothly as we are able to speak, they take it as an almost insufferable injury unless the applause is so predominant as to drown all the force of the reproof or confutation.

Brethren, I know this is a sad and harsh confession. But that all this should be so among us should be more grievous to us than to be told of it, and I desire to deal closely with my own heart as well as yours. Have not many of us cause to inquire whether sincerity will consist with such a measure of pride? When we are telling the drunkard that he cannot be saved unless he becomes temperate, and the fornicator that he cannot be saved unless he becomes chaste (an undoubted truth), do we not have as great a reason, if we are proud, to say of ourselves that we cannot be saved unless we become humble? Certainly, pride is a greater sin than whoredom or drunkenness, and humility is as necessary as chastity and sobriety.

The work may be God's, and yet we do it not for God but for ourselves. I confess that I feel such continual danger on this point that if I do not watch against it, I would study for myself, preach for myself, and write for myself rather than for Christ, and then my work would surely go amiss. Consider, I beseech you, what baits there are in the work of the ministry to entice a man to be selfish, that is, to be carnal and impious even in the highest works of piety. The fame of a godly man is as great a snare as the fame of a learned man: woe to him who takes up with the reputation of godliness instead of godliness itself. "Verily I say unto you, they have their reward" (Matt. 6:2, 5).

———

Questions for Reflection

1. Baxter says that "this is a sad and harsh confession" (p. 75). Do you think his focus is appropriate or misplaced? Is confession like this too sad or too harsh?

2. Baxter's opening target is pride. Why do you think he begins his confession here?

3. In our own day, it is rare to see anything like this public confession of sin. Why do you think we have lost this practice? Should we restore it?

4. Pride is a "subtle" opponent that can dress itself up in the most pious appearance. Can you discern traces of pride in your own heart and ministry?

5. Is your ministry too much about you? Are you too sensitive to your own reputation? Do you bristle when others do not speak highly of you? Are you defensive in the face of criticism?

Many Things Sadly out of Order

Baxter begins his confession with the sin of pride, but he does not end there. He goes on to confront his fellow ministers with their further sins: undervaluing church unity, laziness and negligence in pastoral ministry, and a lack of generosity toward the poor. These are hard words that he urges his fellow ministers to receive with humility and to follow with a new diligence in ministry.

———

AMONG THE MANY THINGS that are still sadly out of order in the best of ministers, pride is the first, but I will also touch on these other particulars following.

Undervaluing Unity

Another sin that the ministers of England are sadly guilty of is undervaluing the unity and peace of the whole church. Though I have hardly ever met a minister who did not speak for unity and peace, yet is it not common to meet with any who are dedicated to promote it. We too commonly find men averse to it and jealous of it. Often they themselves are instruments of division. How rare it is to meet a man who hurts or bleeds with the church's wounds, or movingly takes them to heart as his own, or ever had thoughtful suggestions for a cure. Instead, almost every party thinks that the happiness of the rest consists only in turning to them. Because other parties are not of the same mind, they cry, "Down with them," and are glad to hear of their fall, thinking that their fall is the way to the church's rising (by which they mean their own rising).

How few there are who understand the true state of the controversies between the different parties. Not many see how most of our disputes concern words only and not real differences. Few men become zealous for peace until they grow old or have gained sufficient experience of men's spirits and principles and can see the true state of the church and the various differences between the parties better than they did before. All men confess the worth of peace, and most of them will preach for it and talk for it, yet they sit still and neglect it as if it were not worth seeking. They will read and preach on texts like Romans 12:18 that command men to follow peace with all men as far as possible, yet they are far from following this command and doing all that they possibly can for it. Too many ministers snarl at it and malign and censure anyone who endeavors to promote it, as if all zeal for peace proceeded from an abatement of our zeal for holiness. It is as if holiness and peace had so fallen out with each other that there can be no reconciling them, but long experience has shown that concord is a sure friend to piety, and piety always moves to concord. We have seen how errors and heresies breed from discord, just as discord is bred and fed by them.

The servants of God should live together as one, of one heart and one soul (Acts 4:32). They should promote each other's faith and holiness, admonish and assist each other against sin, and rejoice together in the hope of their future glory. Instead, we have lived in mutual jealousies and drowned holy love in bitter contention. We have studied how to disgrace and undermine one another and to increase our own parties by right or wrong. We used to glory in our love to the brethren as the certain mark of our sincerity in the faith (John 13:35); we have now turned it into a love of our party only, and those who are against our party have more of our bitterness, envy, and malice than our love. It is not only ourselves who are scorched in this flame. We have drawn our people into it so that most of the godly in the nation have fallen into different parties and have turned much of their old piety into vain opinions, disputes, envies, and animosities. Thus we proceed in a contentious zeal to divide the church and censure our brethren and to make the differences between us seem greater than they are, even while we do not know well what they are ourselves, who so eagerly manage them.

Negligence and Lack of Effort

The next sin that I will mention is this: we do not so seriously, unreservedly, and industriously lay out ourselves in the work of the Lord as is appropriate for men of our profession and undertaking. I bless the Lord that there are so many who do his work with all their might! But alas, for the most part, even of those we take for godly ministers, how reservedly and how negligently do we go through our work! How few of us behave ourselves in our office as those who are wholly devoted to unity and who have devoted all that they have to the same ends! I will mention to you some of the sinful discoveries of it, which do too much abound, so that you may see my grounds for this confession.

1. It is too common with us to be negligent in our studies, and few men will take those pains necessary for the right informing

of their understanding and fitting it for their further work. Some men have no delight in their studies. They take only an hour now and then as an unwelcome task that they are forced to undergo, and they are glad when the yoke is removed. Consider the natural desire of knowing, the spiritual desire of knowing God and things divine, the consciousness of our great ignorance and weakness, and the sense of the weight of our ministerial work: Will none of these keep us closer to our studies and make us more careful in seeking after the truth?

Oh, what abundance of things there are that a minister should understand! What a great defect is it to be ignorant of them, and how much will we miss such knowledge in our work! Many ministers study only to compose their sermons and very little more, when there are so many books to be read and so many matters that we should be acquainted with. In the preparation of our sermons, we are too negligent, gathering only a few bare headings and not considering the most forcible expressions by which we should set them home to men's hearts. We must study how to convince and get within men and how to bring each truth to the heart and not leave all this to the spur of the moment (except in cases of necessity). Brethren, experience will teach you that men are not made learned or wise without hard study, unwearied labors, and experience.

2. If ministers were devoted to the work of the Lord, it would be done more vigorously than it is by most of us. How few ministers preach with all their might or speak about everlasting joy or torment in such a manner as may make men believe that they are in good earnest. It would make a man's heart ache to see a company of dead and drowsy sinners sit under a minister and not have a word that is likely to enliven or awaken them. Alas, we speak so drowsily or gently that

sleepy sinners cannot hear. The blow falls so light that hard-hearted persons cannot feel it.

Most ministers will not so much as strain their voice and stir themselves up to an earnest utterance. And when they do speak loudly and earnestly, how few answer it with earnestness of matter! The voice alone does little good. The people will take it but as mere bawling when the force of our preaching does not correspond to the loudness of our voice. It grieves me whenever I hear ministers preach excellent doctrine but let it die in their hands for lack of close and lively application. What fit matter they have for convincing sinners, but how little they make of it. What a deal of good it might do if it were driven home, and yet they cannot or will not do it. Oh, how plain, how close, and how earnestly should we deliver a message of such a nature as ours when the everlasting life or death of men is concerned in it! There is nothing more unsuitable to such a business than to be slight and dull. Should we speak coldly for God and for men's salvation! Can we believe that our people must be converted or condemned and yet speak in a drowsy tone? In the name of God, labor to awaken your hearts before you come to preach and when you are in the work so that you may be fit to awaken the hearts of sinners. Remember that they must be awakened or damned, and a sleepy preacher will hardly awaken them. If we are commanded whatever our hand finds to do, to do it with all our might (Eccles. 9:10), then certainly such a work as preaching for men's salvation should be done with all our might.

3. The negligent execution of acknowledged duties shows that we are not so wholly devoted to the work as we should be. If any business for the church is afoot, how many neglect it for their own private business? When we consult together for the unanimous and successful performance of our work, one minister has this business

of his own and another that business, which must be preferred before God's business. When a work is likely to prove difficult and costly, how backward are we to do it!

For instance, what has been more talked of, prayed for, and contended about in England for many years past than the business of church discipline? Yet when we come to the practice of it, as far as I can see, most of us are for no way of discipline at all. It has made me marvel sometimes to look on the face of England and see how few congregations in the land have any considerable execution of discipline, and why is this? The great reason as far as I can learn is the difficulty of the work and the trouble or suffering that we are likely to incur by it. They say, "We cannot publicly reprehend one sinner but he will storm at it and bear us a deadly malice. We can prevail with very few to make a public profession of true repentance. If we proceed to excommunicate them, they will be raging mad against us. They will be ready to vow revenge against us and to do us mischief, even to the hazard of our lives. Men will not hear us when they hate us. Therefore, duty ceases to be duty to us, because the hurt that would follow would be greater than the good."

These are the great reasons for the nonexecution of discipline, together with the great labor that the private admonition of each offender would cost us. But let me tell you that there is not such a lion in the way as you imagine (Prov. 26:13), nor is discipline such a useless thing. I bless God for the small and too-late trial that I have made of it myself. I can speak by experience: it is not vain, nor are the hazards of it such as may excuse our neglect.

Selfish Use of Our Money

There is another sad discovery that we have not devoted ourselves and all we have to the service of God as we ought to do: it is the prevalence of worldly, fleshly interests too much against the interest and work of Christ. Experience has fully proved that works of charity most potently remove people's prejudice and open their ears to words of piety. When they see that you love them and seek their good, they will the more easily trust you. When they see that you do not seek the things of the world, they will the less suspect your intentions and be more easily drawn by you to seek that which you seek. Oh, how much good might ministers do if they set themselves wholly to do good and if they dedicated all their faculties and substance to that end. Do not say that it is a small matter to do good to men's bodies and that this will merely win them to us and not to God, nor convert the soul. For it is prejudice that is a great hindrance of men's conversion, and this will remove it. Do not think that it is ordinary charity that is expected from you any more than ordinary piety.

I know the great objection is this: "We have wife and children to provide for. A little will not serve them at present, and we are not bound to leave them beggars." To which I answer:

1. There are few texts of Scripture more abused than that of the apostle in 1 Timothy 5:8: "If any provide not for his own, especially those of his house, he has denied the faith and is worse than an infidel." This is made a pretense for providing a full inheritance for posterity when the apostle speaks only against those who cast their poor kindred and family on the church to be maintained out of the common fund when they were able to do it themselves. His following words show that it is present provision and not future portions that he speaks of when he bids those who have widows to give them what is sufficient (1 Tim. 5:16).

2. You may educate your children as other poor persons do, so that they can earn their own income in some honest trade or employment,

all without other great provisions. I know that your charity and care must begin at home, but it must not end there. You are bound to do the best you can to educate your children so that they may be capable of being most serviceable to God, but you are not bound to leave them rich or with a full inheritance. Nor should you forsake other necessary works of charity merely for a larger provision for your children. We must keep some proportion between our provision for our families and for the church and poor. A truly charitable, self-denying heart that has devoted itself and all that he has to God would be the best judge of the due proportions and would see which way of expense is likely to do God the greatest service, and that is the way he would take.

3. I confess that I would not have men lie too long under endangering, strong temptations by remaining unmarried, lest they wound themselves and their profession by their falls, but can men not do more to mortify the desires of the flesh so that they may live in a single, freer condition? Then they would have none of these temptations from wife and children to hinder them from furthering their ministerial ends by charitable works. If he who does not marry does better than he who does (1 Cor. 7:38), surely ministers should labor to do that which is best.

Oh, brethren, what abundance of good works are before us, and how few of them do we put our hands to! I know the world expects more from us than we have. But if we cannot meet the expectations of the unreasonable, let us do what we can to answer the expectations of God, conscience, and all just men. It is the will of God that with well doing we should "put to silence the ignorance of foolish men" (1 Pet. 2:15).

I will proceed no further in these confessions and discoveries but beseech you to take what I have said into consideration. See whether this is not the great and lamentable sin of the ministers of the gospel: they are not fully devoted to God. They do not give themselves and all that they have to accomplishing the blessed work that they have undertaken. See whether flesh pleasing, self-seeking, and an interest distinct from that of Christ make us neglect much of our duty and walk too unfaithfully in so great a trust. See whether we reservedly serve God in the cheapest and most applauded part of his work and withdraw from that which would put us to cost and suffering. See whether too many are earthly who seem to be heavenly, and mind the things below while they preach the things above, and idolize the world while they call men to hate it.

The Appropriateness of Confession

And now, brethren, what remains but that we all cry "Guilty!" of too many of these sins and humble our souls in the lamentation of our failure before the Lord. Are we taking heed unto ourselves and to all the flock? Do we follow the pattern that is given to us here in Acts 20? If we now prove hard-hearted, unhumbled men and sniff at these confessions as tending to our disgrace, how sad a symptom would it be to ourselves and to the church? The ministers of England are not the least or last in the sin of the land. They have encouraged the common profaneness. They have led their people into divisions and are now too reluctant to bring them out. As sin has been found in them, so judgments have been found and laid on them.

Therefore, it is time for us to take our part in that humiliation to which we have been calling our people for so long. If we have our wits about us, we may perceive that God has been offended with us and that the voice that called this nation to repentance spoke to us as well as to others. Judgment has begun at the house of God (1 Pet. 4:17). If humiliation does not begin there, too, it will be a sad condition to us and to the land. What? Shall we deny, excuse, or extenuate our sins while we call our people to such free confessions? Is it not better to give glory to God by a full and humble confession than in tenderness of our own glory to seek for fig leaves to cover our nakedness (Gen. 3:7)?

Imagine that one among your hearers on a day of humiliation, when sin is fully confessed and lamented, is offended at the confession and stands up against you and says, "You wrong me! I am not so bad! You should have told me of this in private and not have disgraced me before the congregation." What would we think of such a man except that he was a hardened, impenitent wretch? Shall we do that which we scarcely ever see the most hardened sinner do? Shall we say, "This should not have been spoken about us in the ears of the people, but we should have been honored before them"? We have committed our sins before the sun so that they cannot be hidden. Attempts to cloak them increase our guilt and shame. There is no way to repair the breaches in our honor that our sin has made except by free confession and abasement. I am compelled to make confession of my own sins, and if anyone is offended that I have confessed theirs, let them know that I do only what I have done for myself. If they dare disown the confession of their sin, let them do so at their peril. But as for all the truly humble ministers of the gospel, I am sure they would rather be provoked more solemnly in the face of their congregations to lament their sins and promise reformation.

Questions for Reflection

1. "How few of us behave ourselves in our office as those who are wholly devoted to unity!" (p. 79). To what extent does this describe you? Are you wholly devoted to the work of unity?

2. Baxter targets disunity, negligence, and a lack of charity. Do you share in any of these sins?

3. Is Baxter being too hard on his fellow ministers? While you may know little (if anything) about seventeenth-century England, do you think his general approach is the right one?

4. If you were speaking in Baxter's place today, how would you approach the subject of confession? What general ministerial sins would you identify? What sins do you see in yourself?

5. If you are married and have a family, how do you balance the interests of your family and your ministry?

Reasons Why You Should Take Heed unto All the Flock

Having made a full confession of ministerial sin, Baxter returns to Acts 20:28: "Take heed unto yourselves and all the flock, over which the Holy Spirit has made you overseers, to feed the church of God, which he has purchased with his own blood." He reflects on the role of overseer and the priceless worth of the church for which Christ died. He also offers some advice on how to be effective in preaching and pastoral ministry.

HAVING DISCLOSED AND LAMENTED our sins and neglects, our duty for the future lies plainly before us. God forbid that we should now go on as carelessly as we did before in the sin that we have just confessed. Be awakened, therefore, I beseech you, by the loud and manifold voice of God, to set more seriously to the work of God and to do it for the future with all your might, and to take heed unto yourselves and to all the flock. In the beginning I gave you the reasons why you should take heed unto yourselves. Now I will give you the reasons why you should take heed unto all the flock as motives to enforce this exhortation. The Lord grant that they may work in us according to their truth and weight.

We Are Called to Be Overseers

The first enlivening consideration that Acts 20:28 affords us is taken from our relation to all the flock: we are overseers of it.

1. The nature of the office requires us to take heed. What else are we overseers for? Consider where you stand and what you have taken upon you. You have undertaken the conduct under Christ of a band of his soldiers against principalities, powers, and spiritual wickedness in high places (Eph. 6:12). You must lead them on the sharpest conflicts. You must acquaint them with the enemy's strategies and assault. You must watch yourselves and keep them watching. If you are negligent, they and you may perish. You have a subtle enemy, so you must be wise. You have a vigilant enemy, so you must be vigilant. You have a malicious, violent, and unwearied enemy, so you must be resolute, courageous, and unwearied. You are in a crowd of enemies, surrounded by them on every side, and if you heed only one enemy and not all of them, you will quickly fall.

Oh, what a world of work you have to do! If you have just one ignorant old man or woman to teach, what a tedious task that is even when they are willing to learn. But if they are as unwilling as they are ignorant, how much more difficult is it! And then to have a multitude of such people, as most of us have, what work will it find us! What a world of wickedness we have to contend against in just one soul, and what a number of those worlds! What deep roots have their sins! What disadvantage must truth come upon! When you think you have achieved something in a person, you leave your seed among the fowls of the air (Luke 8:5), and wicked men are at their elbows to rise up and contradict all that you have said. They use weaker reasons than yours, but they come with more advantage for being near them. Weak reasons from familiar friends are strongly urged. They are fetched from things that they see and feel and that are befriended by their own flesh. You speak only once to a sinner for the ten times or twenty times that the messengers of Satan speak to them.

Moreover, how easily do the cares and business of the world devour and choke the seed that you have sown (Luke 8:7). Even if it had no other enemy but what is already there in themselves, how easily will a frozen, carnal heart extinguish those sparks that you have long been kindling! For lack of fuel and further help, they will be extinguished. What abundance of distempers, lusts, and passions you cast your gracious words among, and what entertainment such companions will afford them, you may easily imagine. When you think your work has happily succeeded and you have seen men under troubles and complaints confessing their sins, promising reformation, and living as new creatures and zealous converts, alas, after all this, they may prove unsound and false at heart. They will show that they were but superficially changed. They took up new opinions and new company without a new heart. How many people, after a notable change, are deceived by the profits and honors of the world and have fallen away even while they think they stand? How many are entangled again in their former sensuality? How many merely exchange a disgraceful way of pleasing the flesh for one that is less dishonorable and does not make such a loud noise in their consciences?

2. Consider also that it is by your own voluntary undertaking and engagement that all this work is laid on you. No one forced you to be overseers of the church. Does not common honesty bind you to be true to your trust?

3. Consider the honor that encourages you to the labor. It is indeed a great honor to be the ambassadors of God and the instruments of

men's conversion and salvation, to save men's souls from death, and to cover a multitude of sins (James 5:20).

4. Consider that you have the many other excellent privileges of the ministerial office that encourage you to do the work. If you will not do the work, you can have nothing to do with the privileges. You are maintained by other men's labors and live on a public allowance. This is so that you may not be taken away from your work but, as Paul requires, may give yourselves wholly to these things (1 Tim. 4:15) and not be forced to neglect men's souls while you are providing for your own bodies. Either do the work, or do not take the income.

But you have far greater privileges than even this. Is it nothing to be trained for learning when others work only at the plough and cart? You are furnished with so much delightful knowledge when the world lies in ignorance. Is it nothing to converse with learned men and talk of high and glorious things when others must converse with almost none but silly, ignorant people? What an excellent life it is to live in the studies and preaching of Christ. How excellent to be still searching into his mysteries or feeding on them, to be daily in the consideration of the blessed nature, works, or ways of God! Others are glad of the leisure of the Lord's Day and an hour now and then during the week when they can lay hold of it. But we may keep a continual Sabbath. We may do almost nothing else but study and talk of God and glory, and call on him and drink in his sacred, saving truths. Our employment is all high and spiritual! Whether we are alone or with others, our business is for another world. If only our hearts were more suitable to this work, what a blessed, joyful life should we live! How sweet would our study be to us to live among such excellent helps as our libraries afford and to have so many silent, wise companions whenever we please and of such variety. These are the privileges of the ministry. All these and more call forth our unwearied diligence in the work.

5. You are the stewards of Christ's mysteries and rulers of his household, and he that entrusted you with his work will maintain you in it, but it is required of a steward that he be found faithful (1 Cor. 4:2). Be true to God, and never doubt that he will be true to you. As you feed his flock, he will feed you, just as he fed Elijah (1 Kings 17:6).

The Worth of God's Church

It is God by his Spirit who makes us overseers of his church, and if our commission is sent from heaven, it is not to be disobeyed. When Paul was called by the voice of Christ, he was not disobedient to the heavenly vision (Acts 9:1–9). When the apostles were called by Christ from their secular employments, they immediately left their friends, house, trade, and all to follow him (Matt. 19:27). Though our call is not so immediate or extraordinary, yet it is from the same Spirit. It is no safe course to imitate Jonah, in turning our back on the commands of God.

It is the church of God that we must oversee and feed. It is that church that is sanctified by the Holy Spirit, is united to Christ, and is his mystical body. Oh, what a charge it is that we have undertaken! Shall we be unfaithful to such a charge? Have we been given the stewardship of God's own family, and shall we neglect it? God forbid! Christ walks among them. Remember his presence and keep all as clean as you can. The praises of the Most High God are in the midst of them. They are a sanctified, chosen people, a kingly priesthood, a holy nation, a choice generation, to show forth the praises of him who has called them (1 Pet. 2:9).

Remember the price that was paid for the church that we oversee. As Paul says in this very text, God the Son purchased the church with his own blood. Oh, what an argument this is to enliven the negligent, and what an argument to condemn those who will not be awakened to their duty by it! Shall we despise the blood of Christ? Shall we think it was shed for those who are not worthy of our utmost care? Then let us hear those arguments of Christ whenever we feel ourselves grow dull and careless: "Did I die for them, and will you not look after them? They were worth my blood, and are they not worth your labor? Did I come down from heaven to earth, to seek and to save that which was lost (Luke 19:10), and will you not go to the next door or street or village to seek them? How small is your labor or humbling in comparison to mine! I debased myself to this, but it is your honor to be so employed. I have done and suffered so much for their salvation, and I have made you a coworker with me, and will you refuse the little that lies upon your hands?" Every time we look on our congregations, let us believingly remember that they are the purchase of Christ's blood and that we should regard them as such.

How to Prosper in This Work of Overseeing

A further exhortation is this: be very careful that you keep your own faith in life and action and that you preach to yourselves before you preach to others. If you did this for your own sakes, it would be no lost labor, but I am speaking to you for the sake of the church. When your minds are in a heavenly, holy frame, your people partake of the fruits of it. Your prayers, praises, and doctrine will be heavenly and sweet to them. They will feel it when you have been much with God: that which is most on your hearts is likely to be most in their ears. I confess that I must speak it by lamentable experience that when I let my heart grow cold, my preaching grows cold. When my heart is confused, my preaching will be also. I observe it too often in the best of my hearers that when I have for a little while grown cold in preaching, they have cooled accordingly, and the next prayers that I have heard from them have been too much like my preaching.

We are the nurses of Christ's little ones (1 Thess. 2:7). If we neglect our food, we will starve them. They will quickly find it in the lack of milk, and we may quickly see it in the lean and dull discharge of their various duties. If we let our love go down, we are not as likely to raise theirs up. If we abate our holy care and fear, it will appear in our doctrine. If the matter does not show it, the manner will. Keep watch, therefore, over your own hearts. Keep out lusts, passions, and worldly inclinations; keep up the life of faith and love. Be much at home, and be much with God. If it is not your daily, serious business to study your own hearts, subdue corruptions, and live on God, and if you do not make it the work to which you constantly attend, all will go amiss. Above all, be much in secret prayer and meditation. There you must fetch the heavenly fire that must kindle your sacrifices. Remember you cannot decline and neglect your duty to your own hurt alone, but many will be losers by it as well as you. For your people's sakes, therefore, look to your hearts.

My next particular exhortation is this: stir yourselves up to the great work of God when you are upon it, and see that you do it with all your might (Eccles. 9:10). I do not urge you to a constant loudness (for that will make your fervency contemptible), but make sure you have a constant seriousness. When the matter requires it (as it should do in the application of every doctrine), then lift up your voice, spare not your spirits, and speak to the people as to men who must be awakened either here or in hell. Look on your congregations believingly and with compassion, and think in what a state of joy or torment they must all be forever. It will make you earnest and melt your heart to imagine their condition. Do not speak one cold or careless word about so great a business as heaven or hell! Whatever you do, let the people see that you are sincere and earnest. Truly, these are great works to be done, and you must not think that trifling will fulfill them.

Another great matter lies in our pronunciation and tone of speech. The best matter will hardly move our hearers if it is not movingly delivered. In particular, make sure that there is no affectation but that we speak to our people as we would do if we were talking to any of them personally. The lack of a familiar tone and expression is as great a defect in most of our preaching as anything whatsoever and that which we should be very careful to amend. When a man has a reading or formal tone, like a schoolboy saying his lesson, few are moved with anything that he says. Let us, therefore, rouse ourselves up to the work of the Lord and speak to our people as for their lives.

Moreover, if you would prosper in your work, be sure to keep up earnest desires and expectations of success. If your hearts are not set on the end of your labors and you do not long to see the conversion and edification of your hearers and do not study and preach in hope, you are not likely to see much fruit of it. It is a sign of a false, self-seeking heart that it can be content to be working and yet see no fruits of its labor. I have observed that God seldom blesses any man's work so much as those whose heart is set on success. No wise or charitable physician is content to be still giving medicine and see no amendment among his patients but have them all die under his care. Nor will any wise and honest schoolmaster be content to be still teaching though his students fail to profit. Both physician and schoolmaster would instead be weary of the employment. Of course, I know that a faithful minister may have comfort when he lacks success, that our reward is with the Lord, and that our acceptance is not according to the fruit but according to our labor.

Do not just say well, but do well. Be zealous for good works. Spare not any cost if it may promote your Master's work. Maintain your innocence, and walk without offense. Let your lives condemn sin and persuade men to duty. Would you have your people be more careful of their souls than you are of yours? If you would have them redeem their time (Eph. 5:16), do not misspend yours. If you would not have them waste their time in idle conversation, make sure that you speak yourselves only of those things that may edify and that tend to minister grace to the hearers. Order your own families well if you would have them do so in theirs. Do not be proud and lordly if you want them to be lowly. There is no virtue wherein your example will do more good than humility, meekness, and self-denial. Forgive injuries. Do not be overcome by evil, but overcome evil with good (Rom. 12.21). Do as our Lord did: when he was abused, he did not return abuse (1 Pet. 2:23). When sinners are stubborn and contemptuous, flesh and blood will tempt you to take up their weapons and to master them by their carnal means, but that is not the way. Overcome them with kindness, patience, and gentleness.

———

Questions for Reflection

1. What do you think it means to be an overseer in the church of God? What responsibilities come along with it?

2. "These are great works to be done," says Baxter, "and you must not think that trifling will fulfill them" (p. 96). Do you give everything you should to the oversight with which God has entrusted you?

3. How do you see the church? It is all too easy to see only its flaws and failings. How does your perspective on ministry change when you see the church as Baxter sees it, comprising those for whom Christ died?

4. Baxter clearly had a deep appreciation for books, his "many silent, wise companions" (p. 92). Do you? What do these companions offer, and how can they enrich your ministry?

5. Baxter draws a direct connection between the liveliness of our own faith and the liveliness we see in our people. Do you accept that there is a connection? Are there patterns you need to change in order to maintain a vibrant faith for the sake of your people?

The Greatest Benefits of Our Work

Baxter well knew the cost and labor of providing individual instruction to every person under his pastoral care. He also knew the benefits that grew out of this costly practice and how those benefits motivated him to continue in the work. He now shares fifteen of those benefits with his fellow ministers.

―――

BRETHREN, WILL YOU FAITHFULLY discharge the great duty that you have undertaken in personally catechizing and instructing everyone in your parishes who will submit to it? Because this is the chief business of the day, I must insist somewhat the longer on it. I will give you some further motives to persuade you to faithfulness in the undertaken work.

The Call to Private Instruction

The first reasons by which I will persuade you to this duty are taken from the benefits of it. When I consider what this work well managed is likely to produce, through the blessing of God, it makes my heart leap for joy. Truly, brethren, you have begun a most blessed work that your own consciences may rejoice in, your parishes rejoice in, and the nation rejoice in. Even the child that is yet unborn will rejoice in it. Indeed, for ought we know, thousands and millions may yet have cause to bless God when we have finished our course.

Though it is our business here to humble ourselves for the neglect of this duty for so long, as we have very great cause to do, yet the hopes of blessed success are so great in me that they are ready to turn it into a day of rejoicing. I bless the Lord that I have lived to see such a day as this and to be present at so solemn an engagement of so many servants of Christ to such a work. I bless the Lord that he has honored you to be the beginners and awakeners of the nation in this great work.

Because the work in hand is so pregnant with great advantages to the church, I will come down to the particular benefits that we may hope for. When you see the excellence of it, you will be more set on it and more reluctant by any negligence or failing to destroy or frustrate it. Certainly, he who has the true intentions of a minister will rejoice in the appearance of any further hopes of attaining his ends, and nothing can be more welcome to him than that which will further the very business of his life. I will show you that our present work is such, in these particulars.

Fifteen Benefits of Private Instruction

1. We cannot expect a more hopeful advantage for the conversion of many souls than private instruction. Oh, brethren, what a blow we may give the kingdom of darkness by the faithful and skillful managing of this work! If the saving of souls, of your neighbors' souls, of many souls from everlasting misery is worth your labor, get up and be doing! If you are indeed coworkers with Christ (1 Cor. 3:9), then set to his work and do not neglect the souls for whom he died.

2. The second happy benefit of our work, if well managed, will be the most orderly building up of those who are converted and the establishing of them in the faith. It risks the whole work, or at least much hinders it, when we do not do it in the order that it must be done. How can you build if you do not first lay a good foundation? How can you put the capstone in place while the middle parts are neglected? The second order of Christian truths have such dependence on the first that they can never be well learned until the first are learned. Therefore, the most godly people in your congregations will find it worth their labor to learn the words of a catechism. If you would safely edify them and firmly establish them, be diligent in this work.

3. A third benefit that may be expected by the well managing of this work is that it will make our public preaching better understood and regarded. When you have acquainted the people with the principles, they will better understand all that you say. Once they are acquainted with the foundation, they will perceive what you drive at. This acquaintance prepares their minds and opens a way to their hearts. If you would not lose the benefit of your public labor, make sure that you are faithful in this private work.

4. When you have had the opportunity of a personal conference, you will come to be familiar with your people. The lack of this close engagement for those of us with very large parishes is a great impediment to the success of our labors. By our distance and unacquaintedness, slanderers and deceivers have the opportunity to possess our people with false conceptions of us that prejudice their minds against our doctrine. By this distance and strangeness, abundance of misunderstandings between ministers and their people develop. Besides that, familiarity itself tends to nurture those affections that may open their

ears to further teaching. When we are familiar with them, they will be more encouraged to be open about their doubts, seek resolution, and deal freely with us. But when a minister does not know his people or is as strange to them as if he did not know them, it must be a great hindrance to his doing them any good.

5. By means of private instruction, we will come to be better acquainted with each person's spiritual state, and so we will better know how to watch over them and carry ourselves toward them ever after. We will know better how to preach to them when we know their disposition and their chief objections and thus what they most need to hear. We will better know how to lament for them and rejoice with them and how to pray for them to God. Just as he who will pray rightly for himself will know his own sores and the diseases of his own heart, so he that seeks to pray rightly for others should know their hearts as far as he may and is appropriate. If a man has the charge merely of sheep or cattle, he cannot well discharge his trust if he does not know them, along with their state and qualities. So it is with the master who will teach his students well and with parents who will rightly educate their children. So it is with us.

6. This acquaintance with our people's state will better satisfy us in the administration of the sacraments. We will better understand how far each person is fit or unfit to receive them.

7. We will by this means be better enabled to help our people against their particular temptations. We will much better prevent their entertaining any particular errors or heresies or their falling into schism to the hazard of themselves and the church, for men will more freely open their thoughts and scruples to us. If they are infected already or inclined to any error or schism, they will be more ready to reveal it. Thus they may receive satisfaction before they are past

curing. Familiarity with their teachers will encourage the people to open their doubts to them at any time.

8. One of the greatest benefits of our work is that it will better inform men of the true nature of the ministerial office or awaken them to a better understanding of it than is now usual. It is now too common for men to think that the work of the ministry is nothing more than to preach well, to baptize and administer the Lord's Supper, and to visit the sick. For this reason the people will submit to no more than that, and too many ministers are negligently or willfully such strangers to their own calling that they will do no more than that. But I do not doubt that through the mercy of God, the restored practice of personal oversight will convince many ministers that this is as truly their work as that which they do now. It may awaken them to see that the ministry is another kind of business than too many excellent preachers take it to be.

9. Another singular benefit that we may hope for from the faithful performance of this work is that it will help our people better understand the nature of their duty toward their overseers and consequently to discharge it better. This would not matter if it were only for our sakes, but their own salvation is very much concerned in it. I am confident by sad experience that it is one of the main impediments to their happiness and to a true reformation of the church that the people do not understand what the work and power of a minister is and what their own duty toward them is. They commonly think that a minister has no more to do with them than to preach to them, visit them in sickness, and administer the sacraments. So if they hear him and receive the sacraments from him, they think that they owe him no further obedience and that he cannot require anything more of them. Little do they know that the minister is in the church as the

schoolmaster is in his school, to teach and to take account of everyone individually, and that all Christians ordinarily must be disciples or students in some such school, for their good.

10. Another benefit is that it may facilitate the ministerial service to the next generation and prevent the rebellion of people against their teachers. As I said, custom is the thing that sways much with the multitude, and those who first break a destructive custom must bear the brunt of their indignation. Someone must do this; if we do not, it will lie on our successors. How can we expect that they should be more hardy, resolute, and faithful than we are? But if we who are set in the front would now break through and break the ice for those who follow, their souls will bless us, our names will be dear to them, and they will feel the happy fruits of our labor every week and every day of their ministry. Thus we may do much for the saving of many thousands of souls in all ages to come as well as in the present age that we are working in.

11. Another benefit is that we will keep our people's minds and use of time from much of that vanity that now possesses them. When men are at work in their shops, almost all their talk is vanity. The children also learn foolish and crude songs and tales, and with such filth and rubbish their memories are furnished. Many an hour is lost, and they are guilty of many a thousand idle thoughts and words. But if they know that the catechism must be learned and that they will soon be asked to repeat it, this will turn much of their thoughts and time that way.

12. It will do much for the better ordering of families and better spending of the Lord's Day. When the master of the family agrees that he will once every Lord's Day examine his family and hear what they can say of the catechism, it will find them the most profitable employment. Otherwise, many masters would be idle or ill employed.

13. It will do some good to many ministers who are apt to be too idle and to misspend their time in unnecessary conversations, business, journeys, or recreations. It will let them see that they have no time to spare for such things. It will be the best cure for all their idleness or loss of time when they are engaged in so much pressing employment of so high a nature.

14. Many personal benefits will come to us as a consequence of these. It will do much to exercise and increase the inner workings of God's grace in our own lives and to subdue our own corruptions. Besides our safety, it will breed much peace in our own consciences and comfort us when our time and actions must be reviewed.

15. We will see the reforming and saving of people in our many parishes, for we will not leave out any man who will submit to be instructed. Though we can scarcely hope that every person will be reformed and saved by it, yet we have reason to hope that as the attempt is universal, so the success will be more general or extensive than we have seen from our other labors up until now. It is likely to be a work that will reach over the whole land and not stop with us who have now engaged in it. Oh, what a happy thing to see all England so seriously called on and urged on for Christ and set in so fair a way to heaven! The consideration of it should make our hearts rejoice within us, to see so many faithful servants of Christ all over the land engaging with every individual sinner with such painstaking appeals for the saving of their souls. I think I even see all the godly ministers of England setting upon the work already and resolving to take the opportunity. Their unanimity may facilitate it, and God will give them success. Is it not, then, a most happy undertaking that you are all setting your hands to and desiring the assistance of Christ in this day?

Undertaking this work of personal instruction is the best way to answer the judgments, the mercies, the prayers, the promises, the cost, the endeavors, and the blood of the Reformation. Without this, the Reformation will not be completed. The ends of all these labors will never be well attained, and an effective reformation will never be brought about. The church will still be low, and the interest of Christ will still be much neglected. God will still have a controversy with the land and, above all, with the ministers who have been deepest in the guilt. Dear brethren, it is you and such as you who under Christ must give this nation the fruit of all the prayers of the Reformers, their cares, their works, their cost, their blood, and their heavy sufferings. All that they did for the good of the church and for true reformation for so many years was only to prepare the way for you to come in and do the work that they desired. They have opened the door for you. At exceeding cost and suffering, they have removed many of your impediments and put the building instruments into your hands. Will you now stand still and loiter? God forbid! Up then, brethren, and give the nation the fruit of their cost and pains. Do not now frustrate all the preparers' work. Do not fail the long expectations of so many thousands who have prayed in hope of a true reformation. They have paid in hope, ventured in hope, suffered in hope, and waited until now in hope. In the name of God, take heed that now you do not fail all these hopes.

———

Questions for Reflection

1. "If the saving of souls, of your neighbors' souls, of many souls from everlasting misery is worth your labor, get up and be doing!" (p. 100). Baxter wrote these words from his parish context in seventeenth-

century England. How does the urgency of "the saving of souls" motivate you in your ministry?

2. Baxter also introduced a generational dimension at a time when he felt the Protestant Reformation in England was advancing. Is there any generational aspect that compels you in your context? Do you have a similar or different vision of the past and the future?

3. Baxter works through fifteen benefits. How do they translate into your context and experience? Which of these benefits do you find most compelling and relevant?

4. What other benefits would you add? How do those benefits motivate you to ensure that you are providing effective soul care for every person under your oversight?

Many Difficulties We Will Find

The benefits that come from actively keeping watch over all the flock are not the only source of motivation that Baxter offers his fellow ministers. For him, the difficulties of the work are also in their own way a motivation for it, difficulties we confront first in ourselves and then in our people. He is also motivated by the work of conversion and driven by the urgent need of sinners for whom death and eternity lie just around the corner.

———

HAVING GIVEN YOU THE FIRST group of motivating reasons, which were drawn from the benefits of personal instruction, I now come to the second group, which are taken from the difficulties. I confess that they might be seen as discouragements rather than motivations if they were taken in isolation or if the work was unnecessary, but the case is otherwise. For difficulties must energize us to greater diligence in a necessary work, and many difficulties we will find, both in ourselves and in our people. Because they are things so obvious that your experience will leave no room for doubting, I will pass over them in a few words.

Difficulties in Ourselves

1. In ourselves there is much dullness and laziness, so there will be much required to get us to be faithful in so hard a work. Like a sluggard in bed (Prov. 6:9) who knows he should rise and yet delays and would stay as long as he can, so do we in the face of duties that our corrupt natures are against and that require the use of all our powers. Thus sloth will tie the hands of many.

2. We also have a man-pleasing disposition that will make us let men perish lest we lose their love and let them go quietly to hell for fear of making them angry with us for seeking their salvation. We are ready to venture on the displeasure of God and venture our people into everlasting misery rather than draw ill will to ourselves. This distemper must be diligently resisted.

3. Some of us also have a foolish bashfulness that makes us very backward to begin with men and to speak plainly to them. We are so modest that we blush to speak for Christ or to contradict the devil or to save a soul, yet we are less ashamed of works that really are worthy of shame.

4. We are so carnal that we are prone by our fleshly interests to be drawn to unfaithfulness in the work of Christ. We fear losing our tithes and income. We fear bringing trouble on ourselves or setting people against us, and many such consequences. All these require diligence for their resistance.

5. The greatest impediment of all is that we are too weak in the faith. When we should set upon a man for his conversion with all our might, we feel the stirrings of unbelief within us raise up actual questionings of heaven and hell, and whether the things that we should earnestly press home are true. Or our belief in them is so weak that it will hardly excite in us a kindly, resolute, and constant zeal. So our whole motion

will be weak, because the spring of faith is so weak. Oh, what need all ministers have for themselves and their work to make sure that their faith (especially their assent to the truth of Scripture and about the joy and torments of the life to come) is sound and lively.

6. Lastly, we commonly have a great deal of unskillfulness and unfitness for this work. Alas, how few know how to deal with an ignorant worldly man for his salvation! Most ministers barely know how to get within him and win upon him or how to shape all conversations according to men's various conditions and tempers. They do not know how to choose the most appropriate subjects and follow them with the holy mixture of seriousness, terror, love, meekness, and evangelical allurements. Oh, who is fit for such a thing! I seriously profess, it seems to me that it is just as hard, if not harder, to converse with a carnal person to bring about a change in him as it is to preach a sermon.

All these difficulties in ourselves should awaken us to a new resolve, preparation, and diligence so that we are not overcome by them and hindered in the work.

Difficulties in Our People

As for our people, we have just as many difficulties to encounter within them.

1. Too many of them will be obstinately unwilling to be taught. They will scorn to come to us, as being too good to be catechized or too old to learn. We must deal wisely with them in public and private, and by the force of reason and the power of love conquer their perverseness.

2. So great is the dullness of many who are willing that they can barely learn even one page of a catechism in a long time. Therefore,

they will stay away, ashamed of their ignorance, unless we are wise and diligent to encourage them.

3. When they do come, so great is their ignorance and their difficulty in understanding that you will find it a hard matter to get them to understand you. If you do not have the skill of making things plain, you will leave them as strange to the subject at hand as they were before you began.

4. You will find it hard to work things upon their hearts so as to make that saving change that is our end and without which our labor is almost lost. Oh, what a block, what a rock is a hardened, carnal heart! How stiffly will it resist the most powerful persuasions. It will hear of everlasting life or death as a thing of nothing! Therefore, if you do not have great seriousness and fervency along with effective material and fitness of expression, what good can you expect? When all is done, the Spirit of grace must do the work. But God and men choose instruments most suitable to the nature of the agent, work, or end. So it is here that the Spirit of wisdom, life, and holiness works not by foolish, dead, or carnal instruments but by such persuasions of light, life, and purity as are most like himself and the work that is to be done.

5. When you have made some desirable impressions on their hearts, if you do not look after them and have a special care for them when they are gone, their hearts will soon return to their former hardness. Their old companions and temptations will work off all that you have done. I only briefly hint at these things that you know so well.

Final Motivations for the Work

The final sort of motivating reasons are drawn from the necessity of the undertaken work. If it were not necessary, the lazy might be discouraged rather than stirred up by all these difficulties. Because I have already been longer than I intended, I will give you only a brief hint of some of the general grounds of this necessity.

1. Every Christian is obliged to do all he can for the salvation of others, but every minister is doubly obliged, because he is set apart for the gospel of Christ and is to give himself wholly to that work (Rom. 1:1; 1 Tim. 4:15). It is needless to question our obligation further when we know that this work is necessary to our people's conversion and salvation and that we are in general commanded to do all that is necessary to those ends as far as we are able.

For my part, I study to preach as plainly and movingly as I can, and yet I frequently meet with those who have been my hearers these eight or ten years who do not know whether Christ is God or man. They are amazed when I tell them the history of his birth, life, and death and of the sending abroad of the gospel, as if they had never heard it before. Of those who know the history of the gospel, how few they are who know the nature of that faith, repentance, and holiness that it requires. Most of them have an ungrounded confidence in Christ, trusting that he will pardon, justify, and save them while the world has their hearts and they live for the flesh. They take this confidence for a justifying faith. I have found by experience that an ignorant man who has been an unprofitable hearer has received more knowledge and remorse of conscience in half an hour's close discourse than he did in ten years of public preaching.

I know that the public preaching of the gospel is the most excellent means of conversion because we speak to many at once, but it is usually far more effectual to preach it privately to an individual sinner. In public, by length and speaking alone, we lose their attention, but when they are conversing with us, we can easily cause them to attend to what we say. Besides that, we can better answer their objections and engage them by their promises before we leave them, which in public we cannot do. I conclude, therefore, that public preaching will not be sufficient. It may be an effectual means to convert many but not as many as this work will do. You may study long and preach to little purpose if you neglect this duty.

2. The necessity is easily shown from Scripture, both from Christ's own example (who used this conversational preaching both with his disciples and with the Jews) and from the apostles' examples (who did the same). When the apostles made a speech of any length, they and the people discussed it together to its conclusion. Peter preached to the Jews in Acts 2 and to Cornelius and his friends in Acts 10. Philip preached to the eunuch in Acts 8, and Paul preached to the jailor in Acts 16 and to many others. Paul preached privately to the Galatian leaders lest he should have run and labored in vain (Gal. 2:2). His earnest charge no doubt includes it when he says, "I charge you, before God and the Lord Jesus Christ, who will judge the living and the dead at his appearing and his kingdom: preach the word, be persistent in season and out of season; reprove, rebuke, exhort with all long-suffering and doctrine" (2 Tim. 4:1–2). Both public preaching and all sorts of private reproofs and exhortations are here required.

3. How these precepts are followed up with promises and threatenings is so well known that I will pass over that point with the rest.

4. This duty also is necessary for the welfare of our people. How much it is conducive to their salvation is evident. Brethren, can you look believingly on your miserable neighbors and not perceive them calling for your help? Can you see them as the wounded man by the side of the road and unmercifully pass by (Luke 10:31)? Can you hear them cry to you, "Come and help us," as the man of Macedonia said to Paul in his vision (Acts 16:9)? Will you refuse them your help?

Imagine that you are entrusted with a hospital in which one patient languishes in one corner, another groans in another corner and cries out, "Oh, help me, pity me for the Lord's sake," and a third is raging mad and would destroy himself and you. Will you sit idle or refuse to offer your help? If you see your brother in need and shut up your compassion from him, how does the love of God dwell in you (1 John 3:17)? You are not such monsters, such hard-hearted men, that you will not pity a leper, you will not pity the naked, imprisoned, or desolate, and you will not pity him who is tormented with grievous pain or sickness. Will you not pity an ignorant, hard-hearted sinner? Will you not pity one who must be shut out from the presence of the Lord and lie under his remediless wrath if a thorough repentance does not speedily prevent it?

5. I must further tell you that this ministerial faithfulness is necessary for your own welfare as well as for your people's. For this is your work according to which (among other works) you will be judged. Let us therefore take time while we have it and work while it is day, for the night comes when no one can work (John 9:4). This is our day, too, and by doing good to others, we will do good to ourselves. If you would prepare for a comfortable death and a sure and great reward, the harvest is before you. Gird up the loins of your minds and conduct yourselves like men so that you may end your days with that confident triumph, "I have fought a good fight, I have finished my course, I have kept the faith. Henceforth there is laid up for me a crown of righteousness, which the Lord, the righteous judge, shall give me at that day" (2 Tim. 4:7–8). Labor now, that you may rest from your labors then.

The God of mercy pardon me and awaken me with the rest of his servants who have been thus sinfully negligent. For I confess to my shame that I seldom hear the bell toll for one who has died, but my conscience asks me, "What have you done for the saving of that soul before it left the body? There is one more gone to judgment; what did you do to prepare him for judgment?" Yet I have been slothful and backward to help the rest who survive. When you are laying a corpse in the grave, how can you not think to yourselves, "Here lies the body, but where is the soul? What have I done for it before it departed? It was part of my charge; what account can I give of it?" Brethren, is it a small matter to you to answer such questions as these? It may seem so now, but the hour is coming when it will not seem so.

———

Questions for Reflection

1. Baxter identifies six likely difficulties within ourselves: laziness, people pleasing, embarrassment, fear, lack of faith, and lack of skill. Do you see any of these difficulties in yourself? What other difficulties stand in your way?

2. There are also obstacles in the people you oversee. What discourages you from providing individual soul care to the people under your charge?

3. Do you agree with Baxter that public preaching is insufficient in itself to bring about the kind of lasting individual change that he has in mind?

4. As you have just read, Baxter thought to himself when a parishioner died, "Here lies the body, but where is the soul? What have I done for it before it departed? It was part of my charge; what account can I give

of it?" (p. 116). Do you ask yourself this kind of question? As you go about your ministry, how do you regularly bring to mind an eternal perspective regarding those you oversee?

5. Leaders are those who "will have to give an account" (Heb. 13:17 ESV). How does that prospect shape the priorities of your ministry?

Some May Object

Few ministers in England practiced the hard work of systematic, comprehensive, individual instruction that Baxter was proposing. He anticipated a great deal of resistance and objection. In this chapter he responds to six potential objections with stern words, and it may be the most confronting section of the whole book. It is important to realize that Baxter is addressing an imagined objector, not the reader. To rebut these objections, he increasingly crams the chapter with biblical allusions to reinforce its scriptural authority, and he hammers his point home by returning to Acts 20.

I WILL NEXT ANSWER some of those objections that backward minds may cast in our way.

Six Objections to Ministers Providing Private Instruction
Objection 1

Some may object that this course will take up so much time that a pastor will have no time to follow his studies. "Most of us are young and raw," they will say, "and have need of much time to improve our own abilities, which this course of action will prohibit."

To which I answer, it is a very desirable thing for a physician to be thoroughly studied in his art, to be able to see the reason for his experiments, and to resolve such difficult controversies as are before him. But if he had the charge of a hospital or lived in a city that had a raging pestilence and was studying when he should be looking after his patients and saving men's lives, I would take that man for a preposterous student. Indeed, I would think him but a civil kind of murderer.

Objection 2

"But this course will destroy the health of our bodies by continually spending our spirits and allowing us no time for necessary recreations. It will wholly lock us up from any civil, friendly visitations so that we can never stir from home or take our delight at home with our friends for the relaxation of our minds. We will seem discourteous and morose to others, and we will tire ourselves. The bow that is always bent will be in danger of breaking at last."

Answer 1. This is merely the plea of the flesh for its own interest. The sluggard says, "There is a lion in the way" (Prov. 26:13). He will not plough because of the cold (Prov. 20:4). If you consult with flesh and blood, you will receive wise reasons like these against any duty of importance that requires self-denial. Who would ever have been burnt at the stake for Christ if this reasoning had been good? Indeed, who would ever have been a Christian?

Answer 2. An hour or half an hour's walk before food is as much recreation necessary for the health of most of the weaker sort of people. I know this by long experience. I have a body that has languished under great weaknesses for many years, and I have found exercise the principal means of my preservation until now. Therefore, I have as great a reason to plead for it as any man that I know alive. Yet I have found that the aforesaid proportion has been blessed to my preservation (though I know that much more would have tended to my greater health).

Answer 3. What is our time and strength for but to lay it out for God? What is a candle made for but to be burnt? Burnt and wasted we must be in the end. Is it not fitter that we should be spent in lighting the way for men to heaven and in working for God than in living for the flesh? How little difference is there between the pleasure of a long life and of a short one when they are both at an end? What comfort will it be at death that you lengthened your life by shortening your work? Oh, precious time! How swiftly it passes away! How soon will it be gone! What are the forty years of my life that are past? Were every day as long as a month, I would think that too short for the work of a day. Have we not lost enough already in the days of our vanity? I never come to a dying man who is not utterly stupid who does not better see the worth of time. If the dying could call time back again, how loud would they call? If they could buy it, what would they give for it? And can we afford to trifle it away? Shall we willfully cast off the greatest works of God? Oh, what a beguiling thing is sin, which can thus distract men who seem so wise! Is it possible that a man of any true compassion and honesty or any care of his ministerial duty or any sense of the strictness of the account he must make before God (Heb. 13:17) should have time to spare for idleness and vanity?

I must tell you further, brethren, that though others may take some time for unnecessary delight, you cannot. Your undertaking binds you more than other men are bound. May a physician in the time of plague take any more relaxation or recreation than is necessary for his life when so many are expecting his help in a case of life and death? His pleasure is not worth men's lives; neither is yours worth men's souls. Imagine your city is besieged: the enemy on one side is watching all advantages to surprise it, and on the other it is seeking to fire it with grenades that are thrown in continually. How much time will you allow these men for their recreation or relaxation whose office is to watch the ports or to quench the fire that will be kindled in the houses? At the most, surely, you would allow them none but what is necessary. Do not begrudge this now and say, "This is a hard saying; who can hear it?" (John 6:60).

Objection 3

"I do not think ministers are required to make drudges of themselves. If they preach diligently, visit the sick, do other ministerial duties, and occasionally do good to those they converse with, I do not think that God requires us to commit ourselves to instruct every person individually and to make our lives a burden and a slavery."

To which I answer, I have showed before how plainly this duty is commanded. Do you think God does not require you to do all the good you can? Will you stand by and see sinners gasping under the pangs of death and say, "God does not require me to make myself a drudge to save them"? Is this the voice of ministerial or Christian compassion, or rather of diabolical cruelty? It is the true character of a hypocrite to make a religion for himself of the cheapest part of God's service that will stand with his fleshly ends and happiness, and to reject the rest that is inconsistent with it. And what a wretched insult this is against the Most High God, to call his service slavery and drudgery! Christ says that he who does not deny himself, does not forsake all, and does not take up his cross and follow him cannot be his disciple (Luke 14:27, 33). How can these men be fit for the ministry who are such enemies to self-denial and thus to true Christianity? Do you not know that it is your own benefit that you begrudge? The more you do, the more you receive; the more you lay out, the more you have coming in. If you are strangers to these Christian paradoxes, you should not have taken it on yourselves to preach them to others.

Objection 4

"But if you make such severe laws for ministers, the church will be left without any ministers. For what man will take on a life of such toil? What parents will choose such a burden for their children? Men will avoid it both for the bodily toil and for the danger to their consciences if they should not fulfill this charge."

Answer 1. It is not we but Christ who has made and imposed these laws that you call severe. If I should silence them or misinterpret them or tell you that there are no such things, that would neither relax them nor disoblige or excuse you. He who made them knew why he did it and will expect us to perform them. Are we to suspect infinite goodness itself of making bad or unmerciful laws? No, it is mere mercy in him that imposes this great duty on us. Must God let the souls of your neighbors perish to save you a little labor and suffering? Oh, what a miserable world should we have, if blind, self-conceited men had the ruling of it?

Answer 2. As for a supply of pastors, Christ will take care of that. He who imposes this duty has the fullness of the Spirit and can give men hearts to obey his laws (Ezek. 36:27). Do you think Christ will suffer all men to be as cruel, unmerciful, fleshly, and self-seeking as you? He who has undertaken himself the work of our redemption, borne our transgressions, and been faithful as the chief shepherd and teacher of the church, will not lose all his labor and suffering for lack of instruments to carry on his work. Nor will he come down again to do all himself because no one else will do it. Instead, he will provide men to be his servants and underteachers in his school who will willingly take the labor on them and rejoice to be so employed and who will account that the happiest life in the world that you account so great a toil. They would not change it for all your ease and carnal pleasure.

Indeed, for the saving of souls and the propagating of the gospel of Christ, they will be content to bear the burden and heat of the day (Matt. 20:12), to fill up the measure of the sufferings of Christ in their bodies (Col. 1:24), to do what they do with all their might (Eccles. 9:10), to work while it is day (John 9:4), to be the servants of all (Mark 9:35), to please not themselves but others for their edification (Rom. 15:2), to become all things to all men so that they may save some (1 Cor. 9:22), to endure all things for the sake of the elect (2 Tim. 2:10), and to spend and be spent for men (2 Cor. 12:15). They will do this even though the more they love, the less they are loved (2 Cor. 12:15), and even though they are considered enemies for telling their people the truth (Gal. 4:16). Christ will provide his people with such pastors after his own heart who will feed them with knowledge (Jer. 3:15).

Objection 5

"But to what purpose is all this when most of the people will not submit? They will scorn your intention. They will tell us that they will not come to us to be catechized and that they are too old now to go to school. Therefore, it is just as good to leave them alone as to trouble ourselves for no purpose."

Answer 1. It is true that too many people are obstinate in their wickedness, too many simple ones love being simple, too many scorners delight in scorning, and fools hate knowledge (Prov. 1:22). But the worse they are, the sadder is their case and the more to be pitied, and the more diligent we should be for their recovery.

Answer 2. Their willfulness will not excuse us from our duty. If we do not offer them our help, how do we know whether they will refuse it? Offering it is our part; accepting is theirs. If we do not offer it, we leave them excusable (for then they have not refused it), and it is we who are left without excuse. But if they refuse our help when it is offered, we have done our part and delivered our own souls (Ezek. 3:19).

Answer 3. If some refuse our help, others will accept it. The success with them may be sufficient to answer all our labor. It is not all who respond to our public preaching, and yet we must not for that reason give up preaching as unprofitable.

Objection 6

"But what likelihood is there that men will be informed or converted by this means who will not be converted by the preaching of the word? That is God's chief ordinance appointed to that end: faith comes by hearing, and hearing by the word preached (Rom. 10:17)."

Answer 1. The advantages I have showed you before (see chap. 7), and therefore I will not take time to repeat them.

Answer 2. I hope there is none so silly as to think that this kind of individual conference is not preaching. Does preaching depend on the number who listen? Is it not preaching when our conversation is with only one man? Surely a man may as truly preach to one as to a thousand. And as I said before (p. 114), gospel preaching in the apostles' days was only occasionally by conference or serious speeches to groups of people but more frequently by asking questions of one or two as opportunity served. Thus Christ himself frequently preached.

Returning to Acts 20

Therefore, there is nothing from God, from the Spirit, or from right reason to cause us to question our work or to be unwilling to do it. But from the world, the flesh, and the devil we will have questions, and more perhaps than we yet expect. If we have recourse to God and look to his great obligations on one side and the hopeful effects and reward on the other, we will see that we have little cause to draw back or to faint (Heb. 10:38).

Let us, then, set before us this pattern in Paul's words from Acts 20, learn our duty, and imitate it. Serve the Lord (not men or ourselves) with all humility of mind (not proudly) and with many tears (20:19). Keep back nothing that is profitable for the people, and teach them publicly and from house to house (20:20). The matter of our preaching should be repentance toward God and faith toward our Lord Jesus Christ (20:21). Though we go bound in the Spirit, not knowing what will befall us but knowing that everywhere afflictions await us, yet none of these things should deter us (20:22–23). Neither should we count our life dear to ourselves, so that we might finish with joy our course and the ministry we have received from the Lord Jesus to testify to the gospel of the grace of God (20:24). Take heed unto ourselves and all the flock, particularly against those grievous wolves, those seducers and schismatics (20:28–30). Never stop warning everyone day and night with tears (20:31). Covet no man's silver, gold, or apparel, counting it more honorable to give than to receive (20:33, 35).

Oh, what a lesson is here before us! But how badly is it learned by those who still question whether all this is their duty. I confess that some of these words of Paul have so often been presented before my eyes and stuck upon my conscience that by them I have been deeply convinced of my duty and convicted about my neglect of this work. I think this one speech better deserves a year's study than most things that young students spend their time studying. Oh, brethren, write it on your study doors, or set it as your text in capital letters still before your eyes. If only we learned even two or three lines of it, what preachers we would be!

Well, brethren, I will spend no more words in exhorting wise merchants to such a bargain or telling teachers themselves of such common truths. If I have said more than needs to be said already, I am glad. I hope now I may take it for granted that you are resolved to apply the utmost diligence and fidelity in the work. I will now proceed on that assumption.

———

Questions for Reflection

1. Baxter asks, "What is a candle made for but to be burnt? Burnt and wasted we must be in the end" (p. 121). Do you agree with Baxter's perspective? Is a shorter but effective life better than a longer but ineffective life?

2. Baxter keeps reworking the image of a physician in a time of plague. Should we feel the same urgency in our ministry? Do you?

3. What kind of reactions do you observe in yourself as Baxter handles each objection? What values can you see at work in what he says? To what extent do you share them?

4. Baxter is not concerned to balance intensity with sustainability in ministry. Is he out of balance, or is there something in his words that

you need to hear? How do you balance intensity and sustainability in ministry?

5. Do you think Baxter's application of Acts 20:18–35 is a reasonable one? Does it mean in practice what he thinks it means? How will you apply these verses in your context?

The Best Directions I Can Give

Over the course of his book, Baxter has worked closely with Acts 20:28; made a confession of sin; explained the benefits, difficulties, and need for individual instruction; and answered objections. Now he brings his work to a close with a very practical application. This chapter presents a series of specific directions about how to encourage people to take part in individual instruction, how to structure each session with them, and how to handle the whole conversation. It supplies a good sense of how Baxter went about his work. The catechism he mentions follows this final chapter.

———

IT IS SO HAPPY A WORK that we have before us that it would be a thousand pities if it were destroyed at its birth and perish in our hands. Though I know that we have a knotty generation to deal with and that it is past the power of any of us to change a carnal heart without the effectual grace of the Holy Spirit, yet it is usual with God to work by means to bless the right endeavors of his servants. Great things will be done and a wonderful blow given to the kingdom of darkness by our undertaken work if it does not miscarry through the fault of the ministers themselves.

The main danger lies in defects of diligence and defects of skill. Against the former, I have spoken much already. As for the latter, I am so conscious of my own unskillfulness that I am far from imagining that I am fit to give directions to any but the younger and more inexperienced ministers. Yet I will say something and not pass over this part in silence, because I am so apprehensive that the welfare of the church and nation very much depends on the management of this work.

How to Bring the People to Us

The best directions that I can give for bringing your people to submit to this course of private catechizing or instruction are these:

1. The chief means of all is for a minister to behave himself in the main course of his ministry and life in a way that tends to convince his people of his ability, his sincerity, and his unfeigned love for them. For if they take him to be ignorant, they will despise his teaching and think themselves as wise as he is. If they think him self-seeking or hypocritical and one who does not mean what he says, they will suspect all that he says and does for them. If they think he intends to domineer over their consciences and to trouble and disgrace them, they will fly away from him as an adversary. But when they are convinced that he understands what he does, and when they have high thoughts of his abilities, they will respect him and more easily stoop to his advice. When they are persuaded of his uprightness, they will be less suspicious of his motives. When they perceive that he intends no private ends for his own benefit but only their good, they will the sooner be persuaded by him.

2. Supposing this general preparation, then, the next thing to be done is to use the most effectual means to convince them of the benefit

and necessity of this course of action to their own souls. The way to win the consent of any man to anything that you offer is to prove it to be good for him and to do this in evidence that is matched to his own understanding. For if you cannot make him believe that it is good or necessary for him, he will never swallow it down but will spit it out with loathing or contempt.

You must therefore preach to the people some effectual, convincing sermons before you begin that will fully show them the benefit and necessity of knowing divine truths in general and of knowing the principles in particular. Tell them that adults have the same duty and need as children and in some respects much more (see Heb. 5:12, which affords us many observations suitable to our present business). Men cannot do their worldly business without knowledge, nor learn a trade without an apprenticeship. Who can love or seek or desire that which he does not know? Convince them what a contradiction it is to be a Christian and yet to refuse to learn. For what is a Christian but a disciple of Christ, and how can he be his disciple if he refuses to be taught by him? He who refuses to be taught by his ministers refuses to be taught by Christ. He will not come down from heaven again to teach them by his own mouth, but he has appointed his ministers to keep school and to teach those under him.

Such an abundance of undeniable evidence is at hand to convince them of their duty. Make them understand that it is not an arbitrary business of our own devising and imposing, but necessity is laid on us. If we do not look to every individual member of the flock according to our power, they may perish in their own iniquities, but their blood will be required at our hands (Ezek. 3:18). Let them know how this has a bearing on their salvation. They will more easily yield to your instruction when they know that it is for their own good.

3. When this is done, you will need to give a copy of the catechism to every family in the parish, poor and rich, so that all might be without excuse. Schedule their visits family by family beginning a month or six weeks after the delivery of the catechism so that they have time to learn it.

4. Be sure that you deal gently with them and take off all discouragements as effectually as you can. Tell them publicly that if they have already learned a different catechism, you will not require them to learn this one. As for the old people who are of weak memories, encourage them to hear the catechism often read over, see that they understand it, and get the matter into their minds and hearts even if they cannot remember the precise words. Let your dealing with those you begin with be so gentle, convincing, and winning that the report of it may encourage others to come as well.

5. If all this will not serve to bring any particular individuals to submit, go to them and discuss the case with them. Know what their reasons are, and convince them of the sinfulness and danger of their contempt for the help that is offered to them. A soul is so precious that we should not lose even one for lack of effort. Keep persuading them while there is any hope, and do not give them up as hopeless until there is clearly no remedy.

How to Be Effective in the Work

Having used these means to procure the people to come in and submit to your teaching, the next thing to consider is how you should deal most effectively with them in the work.

Direction 1. When your people come to you, begin with a brief introduction to soothe and soften their minds and to take off all offense, unwillingness, or discouragement. This will prepare them to entertain your instructions. You might say something like this: "Neighbors, it may perhaps seem an unusual and troublesome business that I put you to, but I hope you will not think it needless. If I thought it were unnecessary, I would have spared you and myself this labor. But my conscience has told me, and God has told me in his word, what it is to be given the trust of overseeing men's souls, and I dare not be so guilty of negligence as I have been. All our business in this world is to get well to heaven, and God has appointed ministers to be guides to his people, to help them get there safely. All other business in the world is like toys and dreams in comparison with this! I hope you will be glad of help in so necessary a work." Something like this may tend to make them more willing to hear you and receive instruction or to give you an account of their knowledge or practice.

Direction 2. When you have spoken thus to them all, take them one by one and deal with them as far as you can in private, out of the hearing of the rest. Some cannot speak freely before others, and some will not endure to be questioned before others, because they think it tends to their shame to have others hear their answers. But the main reason is, as I find by experience, that people will better take plain, close dealing about their sin, misery, and duty when you have them alone than when they are in front of others. If you do not have the opportunity to bring it home and deal freely with them, you will frustrate all. Therefore, if you have enough space, let the rest stay in one room while you confer with each person alone in another room, though for the necessary avoiding of scandal we must speak to the women only in the presence of others.

Direction 3. Take account of what they have learned of the catechism by receiving their answer to each question. If they are able to recite only a little or none of it, see if they can rehearse the Nicene Creed or Apostles' Creed or the Ten Commandments.

Direction 4. Choose some of the most important points in the catechism, and test their understanding by further questions. Do not begin with the less necessary points but with those that they themselves perceive are of the greatest importance to them. Take heed not to ask them intricate, unnecessary, doubtful, or very difficult questions. Deal very tenderly with the common people for matter of knowledge and defect of expression. Some of the most pious, experienced, approved Christians that I know lament to me with tears that they cannot learn the words of the catechism. And they have enjoyed the most excellent assistance in constant duty and in the best company for forty or fifty or sixty years together. This teaches me how little I should expect from poor, ignorant people who never had the benefit of such company or conversation. It reminds me not to reject them so hastily. So if you find such people at a loss and unable to answer your questions, do not drive them on too hard or too long with question after question lest they think you intend only to bewilder them and disgrace them. When you perceive them troubled that they cannot answer, then step in to take the burden off them and offer an answer to the question yourself. Do it thoroughly and plainly, and make a full explanation of the whole business to them, that by your teaching they may be brought to understand it before they leave you.

Direction 5. When you have tested their knowledge, proceed next to instruct them yourselves according to their varied capacities. If it is someone who understands the fundamentals of the faith, give him what you think he most needs. You might explain further some of the mysteries of the gospel, lay the grounds of some duty that he may doubt of, show the necessity of what he neglects, or address his sins and mistakes. Choose what may be most convincing and edifying to him. If it is someone who is grossly ignorant, give him a plain summary of the Christian religion in a few words. Though it may be in the catechism already, a more familiar way may better help him understand it.

Direction 6. If you suspect the person to be unconverted, fall next on a prudent inquiry into his spiritual state. The best and least offensive way will be to take your lead from some point in the catechism and then to proceed with a thought that may soothe the mind by convincing him of the necessity of it. If he says that he hopes he is converted, that all are sinners, or that he is sorry for his sins, then tell him more particularly in a few plain words or by a short description what true conversion is, and so renew and enforce the inquiry.

Direction 7. When you have discerned an apparent probability that the person is still unconverted, your next business is to bring his heart to the sense of his condition with all your skill and power. Set these things home with a more earnest voice than in the former part of your conversation. For if you do not get it into his heart, you do little or nothing. That which does not touch our heart and emotions is soon forgotten.

Direction 8. Conclude the whole conversation with a practical exhortation that must contain the duty of the heart in order to bring about a reconciliation with Christ. Urge the use of external means for the time to come and the avoiding of former sins. If you can, get their promise especially to use means, change their company, and forsake actual sinning, because these are more in their reach. Do this solemnly, reminding them of the presence of God, who hears their promises and will expect the performance (when you have opportunity later on, you can remind them of their promise).

Direction 9. At the dismissing of the people, soothe their minds again with a word like this: "Please do not take it ill that I have put you to this trouble or dealt so freely with you. It brings as little pleasure to me as to you, and if I did not know these things to be true and necessary, I would have spared this labor both to you and to me. But I know that we will be here together only a little while. We are almost at the world to come already, and therefore, it is time for us all to look about us and make sure that we are ready when God calls us." Because we will seldom have opportunity to speak with the same individuals, establish them in a way that will help perfect what is begun. Engage the governor of each family to call all his family to account every Lord's Day before they go to bed, asking them what they can remember of the catechism, and so to keep on doing this until they have all learned it perfectly. When they have done so, he should continue to hear them recite it at least once in two or three Lord's Days so that they will not forget it. For it will be an excellent help even to the most judicious Christian to have in memory a summary of doctrine. If people have learned some small part of the catechism only, make them promise either to come to you again when they have learned the rest or else to go to some able, experienced neighbor to recite it to them and to receive their assistance when you cannot give them time yourself.

Direction 10. If God enable you, extend your charity to those of the poorest sort before they part from you. Give them something toward their relief and for the time they have taken from their labors. Do this especially for the encouragement of those who do best. To the rest, promise them something when they have learned the catechism. I know you cannot give what you do not have, but I speak to those ministers who can.

The Manner of the Whole Conference

Through the whole course of your conversation with them, make sure that the manner as well as the matter is suited to the end. Observe these particulars concerning the manner:

1. Observe the difference of the persons that you have to deal with. To the dull and obstinate, you must be more earnest and sharp. To the tender and timid who are already humbled, you must instead insist on direction and confirmation. To the youthful, you must lay greater shame on sensual sin and show them the nature and necessity of mortification. To the aged, you must do more to disgrace this present world. Make them conscious of the nearness of their death and the aggravations of their sin if they were to live and die in ignorance or impenitence. To inferiors and the younger, you must be more free; to superiors and elders, more reverent. To the rich, this world must be more disgraced and the nature and necessity of self-denial opened. Convey the damnableness of preferring their present prosperity to their future state, together with the necessity of improving their talents in well doing. To the poor, we must show the great riches of glory that is presented to them in the gospel and how well present things may be lost where everlasting things may be gained. Speak particularly against those sins that each one's age, sex, inclination of body, or calling and employment in the world most inclines them to.

2. Be as humble, familiar, and plain as possible with those who are of weaker capacity.

3. Give everyone the Scripture proof and the light of evidence and reason so that they may see that it is not only you but God alongside you who speaks to them.

4. Be serious in everything, especially in the application. I hardly fear anything more than that some careless ministers will hurry over

CHAPTER 10

the work and do all superficially and without life. They will destroy this as they do all other duties by turning it into a mere formality, putting a few cold questions to the people and giving them two or three cold words of advice without any life and feeling in themselves. This is hardly likely to produce any feeling in their hearers. Surely he that values souls and knows what an opportunity lies before him will do this work accordingly.

5. To this end, I think it very necessary both before and during the work that we take special care with our own hearts. We should especially excite and strengthen our belief in the truth of the gospel and in the invisible glory and misery that is to come. I am confident that this work will exceedingly test the strength of our belief. For he who is but superficially a Christian and not sound in the faith will likely feel his zeal quite fail him. In preaching and in other public acts in which there is room for ostentation, such a one will give his best and almost his all. It is another kind of man who must effectually do the private work now in hand.

6. Therefore, it is fitting that we prepare ourselves for this work by private prayer. If time would permit, and if there are many together, it is best if we begin and end with a short prayer with our people.

7. Carry on everything in clear demonstrations of love to your people's souls, and make them feel through the whole that you aim at nothing but their own salvation. Avoid all harsh, discouraging words throughout the conversation.

8. If you do not have time to deal so fully with each one individually as is here directed, do not omit the most necessary parts. Take several of them who are friends and who will not divulge each other's weaknesses, and speak to them together about what concerns them all. Only, the examination of their knowledge and state and of special

directions must be undertaken with the individuals alone. But take heed of hurrying over it (from an unfaithful laziness or from being too brief) without a genuine necessity.

9. Record all the names of your parishioners in a book. Keep a note in your book of who comes and who does not. Note those who are so grossly ignorant as to be utterly incapable of partaking in the Lord's Supper and those who are not. As you perceive the needs of each one, so deal with them in the future.

A Final Encouragement

Well, brethren, I have given you my advice, and I now leave you to the practice. Though the proud may receive it with scorn and the selfish and slothful with some distaste and indignation, I do not doubt that God will use it to awaken many of his servants to do their duty and to promote the work of a right reformation. His great blessing will accompany the present undertaking for the saving of many a soul, for the peace of you who undertake and perform it, and for the purity and the unity of his churches. Amen.

Questions for Reflection

1. Baxter has presented a way of offering individual soul care that worked in his seventeenth-century context. To what extent would it work in yours?

2. In what ways could you take what Baxter has said and rework it for your own context?

3. "I think it very necessary both before and during the work that we take special care with our own hearts" (p. 138). Baxter has in mind our own reluctance and lack of faith, but taking his point more generally, what heart issues are likely to arise as we go about this work? How can we pay close attention to ourselves even as we pay close attention to all the flock?

4. Baxter has brought *The Reformed Pastor* to a close. How would you summarize his essential message in two or three sentences?

5. If you have been at all moved by Baxter's urgency throughout the whole book, what will you now change? How will you implement his vision from Acts 20?

Appendix 1

The Catechism

The catechism was Baxter's main tool in the work of personal instruction. He valued it highly, observing that it would be "an excellent help even to the most judicious Christian to have in memory a summary of doctrine" (p. 136).

What follows is the catechism that Baxter used in his parish. It was published in 1656 at the end of The Agreement of Diverse Ministers of Christ in the County of Worcestershire for Catechizing and Personal Instruction. *It may be useful to see what he was using when he met individually with those under his care.*

Do you think a catechism has merit? It has largely fallen out of favor, but could it still be a useful tool? If you are interested to experiment with the practice, Crossway publishes two contemporary catechisms that you may wish to use in your own ministry: The New City Catechism *(2017) and* To Be a Christian: An Anglican Catechism*, ed. J. I. Packer and Joel Scandrett (2020). You can find further information at https://www.crossway.org/ and http://newcitycatechism.com/.*

Q 1. *What do you believe concerning God?*

A. There is only one God in three persons, the Father, the Son, and the Holy Spirit, who is infinite in being, power, wisdom, and goodness. He is the maker, preserver, and disposer of all things and the most just and merciful Lord of all.

Q 2. *How did God make man, and what law did he give him?*

A. God made man for himself, in his own image, and gave him a righteous law requiring perfect obedience upon pain of death.

Q 3. *Did man keep or break this law?*

A. Man, being tempted by Satan, willfully sinned and so fell from God and happiness to lie under the wrath of God, the curse of the law, and the power of the devil. Thus we are by nature dead in sin and prone to do more evil continually, to grow worse, and to depart even further from God.

Q 4. *How was man redeemed?*

A. God so loved the world that he gave his only Son to be their Redeemer. He, being God and one with the Father, took to himself our nature and became man. He was conceived by the Holy Spirit in the Virgin Mary and born of her and was called Jesus Christ. Having lived on earth without sin and having performed many miracles as a witness to his truth, Jesus gave himself up as a sacrifice for our sins and a ransom for us. After suffering death on the cross and being buried, he rose again on the third day and afterward ascended into heaven, where he is Lord of all in glory with the Father.

Q 5. *How and on what terms is salvation offered in the gospel?*

A. Our Lord Jesus Christ has ordained that all those who receive him by a true, effectual faith; who by true repentance do forsake the devil, the world, and the flesh; and who heartily turn from them to God will freely receive the pardon of their sins and become the sons of God and heirs of everlasting life. If they sincerely love and obey him to the death, they will be glorified. Those who will not do all this will be damned. This he has commanded his ministers to preach to all the world.

Q 6. *How did Christ reveal and prove his doctrine?*
A. The Holy Spirit was sent by the Father and the Son to inspire and guide the prophets, apostles, and evangelists so that they might truly and fully reveal the doctrine of Christ and deliver it in Scripture to the church as the rule of our faith and life. A multitude of miracles provided the great witness to Christ and to the truth of his holy word.

Q 7. *How are men brought to partake of Christ and life?*
A. The same Holy Spirit enlightens men's understandings by the word, softens and opens their hearts, and turns them from the power of Satan to God by faith in Christ. They are joined to Christ, the head, and into one church, which is his body, and are freely justified and made the sons of God, so that they may be a sanctified, chosen people unto him and may overcome the flesh, the world, and the devil. Being zealous for good works, they serve God in holiness and righteousness and live in the special love and communion of the saints in the hope of Christ's coming and of everlasting life.

Q 8. *What will be the end of the righteous and of the wicked?*
A. The Lord Jesus Christ will come again at the end of this world and will raise the bodies of all men from the dead and judge all men according to their works. The righteous will go into everlasting life and the rest into everlasting punishment.

Q 9. *What are the public means that Christ has appointed to salvation?*

A. Christ has appointed that fit men will be ordained his ministers to disciple believers; to baptize all who are disciples in the name of the Father, Son, and Holy Spirit; and to form his disciples into congregations. Christ's ministers are to oversee and guide the various congregations and each individual member of each congregation. His ministers are particularly to teach them the word of God; to pray to and praise God with them and for them; to administer the Lord's Supper in remembrance of him; and to bless them in the name of the Lord. They are especially to do this on the Lord's Day, which he has appointed for holy communion in such works. They are also to rebuke with authority the scandalous and unruly and to reject those who are obstinately impenitent and unreformed.

It is, therefore, the people's duty to join with such churches in the aforesaid worship of God; to know, hear, submit to, and obey those guides who are over them in the Lord; to avoid discord and division; and to live in unity, love, and peace.

Q 10. *What are the secret holy duties that everyone must use?*

A. The secret duties of holiness include frequent and serious meditation on God and on his works and word, especially of our own sin and danger, of our redemption, of our duty, of death and judgment, and of the endless joy or torment after death and judgment. They include the diligent examination of our own hearts and the watching over our thoughts, affections, words, and actions. They include putting to death our sin, especially unbelief, error, hardness of heart, pride, worldliness, flesh pleasing, and hypocrisy. They include the exercise of all graces, watching against temptations, resolutely resisting temptations, and praying secretly to God.

Q 11. *What private duties of holiness must be performed with other people?*
A. The private duties of holiness to be performed with others are these: Parents and masters must teach their children and servants the word and the fear of God, pray with them and for them, and hinder them from sin. Children and servants must willingly learn and obey. We must seek advice in the matters of our salvation, especially from our teachers. We must daily admonish and exhort one another using gracious and edifying conversations and faithful living, confessing our faults to one another, and praying with and for one another. We are to do this especially on the Lord's Day and on other particular occasions of confession or thanksgiving.

Q 12. *What are the necessary duties of righteousness and mercy toward others?*
A. The necessary duties of righteousness and mercy to men are these: Those in authority must rule on behalf of God for the common good with justice and mercy. Those under authority must willingly obey them in the Lord. We must love our neighbors as ourselves and do as we would have others do to us, carrying ourselves toward all others with humility, meekness, harmlessness, sobriety, and truth. We should not wrong anyone in their bodies, chastity, property, or reputation, nor in desire, but we must bear with and forgive one another, loving even our enemies and doing good to all, according to our power.

Appendix 2

Book Outline

Chapter 1: Take Heed unto Yourselves

  A. The importance of taking heed unto ourselves

    1. So that we do not miss the salvation we preach to others

    2. So that we do not live in the sin we preach against in others

    3. So that we have the qualities necessary to perform the work of ministry

    4. So that our practical example does not contradict our doctrine

  B. Why we should take heed unto ourselves

    1. To secure our own salvation first

    2. To guard against our own sinfulness

    3. To preserve us in our greater temptations

    4. To defend ourselves against Satan's attacks

    5. To avoid the spectacle of others seeing us fall

    6. To keep us from heinous sin

    7. To preserve the honor of our Master

    8. To ensure the effectiveness of our work

  C. Reasons why our effectiveness depends on our taking heed

    1. Will God bless those who work only for themselves?

2. Can we pursue that holiness to which our carnal hearts are averse?

3. Can a servant of Satan fight against Satan?

4. Will people listen to a hypocritical preacher?

5. Has God promised to bless the work of the ungodly?

Chapter 2: Take Heed unto All the Flock

  A. The appropriate size of a church

    1. Each congregation should have its own pastor

    2. Each congregation should be no greater than a pastor can take heed of

  B. Taking care of all the flock

    1. The subject matter of the ministerial work

    2. The object of the ministerial work

    3. When we feel our own congregation is too large to take heed of

  C. Recognizing the differences among the flock

    1. Those who are not yet true Christians

    2. Those who are young and weak

    3. Those who labor under troubles

    4. Backsliding Christians

    5. Those who have fallen to temptation

    6. Doubting and disconsolate Christians

    7. Strong Christians who still need our assistance

  D. Putting this into practice

    1. Labor to know our people as well as we can

    2. Use all means possible to instruct the ignorant

    3. Be ready to advise in cases of conscience

    4. Have a special eye on families that they be well ordered

5. Vigilantly oppose seducers

6. Encourage and honor those who are doing well

7. Visit the sick and the dying

8. Comfort the conscience of the troubled

9. Admonish those who continue in sin

10. Practice church discipline

Chapter 3: The Ministerial Work

A. The shape of our work

1. Purely for God and the salvation of our people

2. Laboriously and diligently

3. Prudently, first laying a firm foundation

4. Focusing on the greatest and most necessary things

5. As plainly and as clearly as we can

B. The character we must bring to our work

1. With a sense of our own insufficiency

2. With great humility

3. With a prudent mixture of severity and mildness

4. With an earnest zeal worthy of weighty matters

5. Reverently, as is fitting for the things of God

6. Spiritually, as those led by the Holy Spirit

7. With tender love to our people

8. With patience, even in the face of people's scorn

9. In union and communion with our fellow laborers

Chapter 4: What a Subtle Enemy Is This Sin of Pride!

A. Confessing our sins

1. Scriptural precedents for confession

2. Gratefulness for faithful ministers

B. The particular sin of pride

   1. In how we dress

   2. In how we preach

   3. In guarding our reputation

   4. In defending our opinions

   5. In resenting any rebuke

Chapter 5: Many Things Sadly out of Order

A. Undervaluing unity

B. Negligence and lack of effort

   1. In our studies

   2. In our preaching

   3. In preferring our own interests and concerns

C. Selfish use of our money

   1. The persuasive power of charity

   2. Responding to objections

D. The appropriateness of confession

Chapter 6: Reasons Why You Should Take Heed unto All the Flock

A. We are called to be overseers

   1. Overseers are required to oversee, and what a difficult work it is

   2. We chose to be an overseer; no one forced us to it

   3. There is great honor that comes with the role

   4. There are many privileges that come with the work

   5. A steward is required to be found faithful, and God will be faithful to us

B. The worth of God's church

1. It is the Spirit who calls us to the work
2. These are God's chosen and sanctified people whom we oversee
3. This is the church for which Christ died

C. How to prosper in this work of overseeing

1. Maintain the vibrancy of our own faith and zeal
2. Do the work with a serious fervency
3. Speak to people in a familiar tone of voice
4. Work in the expectation of success, and do not settle for failure
5. Set an example for our people to follow

Chapter 7: The Greatest Benefits of Our Work

A. The call to private instruction

B. Fifteen benefits of private instruction

1. It will bring about the conversion of many souls
2. It will build a firm foundation for those who are already converted
3. It will make our public preaching easier to understand and more effective
4. It will give us a helpful familiarity with our people
5. We will be better acquainted with each person's spiritual state
6. We will know better whom to admit to the sacraments
7. We will be better able to help our people against their particular temptations
8. Our people will become aware of the nature of our office as overseers
9. It will help our people understand their duty toward us
10. We will be setting an example for the next generation of ministers

11. It will help our people make profitable use of their time

12. It will do much for the better ordering of families

13. It will keep ministers from wasting their time

14. We will gain from the work

15. Many people will receive the gospel individually who would not do so otherwise

Chapter 8: Many Difficulties We Will Find

A. Difficulties in ourselves

   1. Our dullness and laziness

   2. Our man-pleasing tendencies

   3. Our embarrassment that holds us back

   4. Our fear of the consequences

   5. Our own weak faith and lack of belief

   6. Our unskillfulness and unfitness for the work

B. Difficulties in our people

   1. Too many are obstinate and unwilling

   2. Others are ashamed of their ignorance

   3. They do not find things easy to understand

   4. Their hearts are hard to change

   5. Their initial change is all too easily lost

C. Final motivations for the work

   1. Public preaching is not enough; our people need individual attention

   2. Christ and the apostles have set us an example

   3. The work comes with both promises and threatenings

   4. The condition of our people should compel us

   5. We will receive commendation or judgment for our work

Chapter 9: Some May Object

  A. Six objections to ministers providing private instruction

    1. The work will take up so much time that we will not be able to study

    2. It will ruin our health

    3. God does not require ministers to make drudges of themselves

    4. If this is what it means to be a minister, no one will want to be a minister

    5. There is no point in even trying this because our people will not submit

    6. Surely preaching is sufficient to convert the people

  B. Returning to Acts 20

Chapter 10: The Best Directions I Can Give

  A. How to bring the people to us

    1. Carry ourselves in such a way that the people see we seek only their good

    2. Convince them of the benefit and necessity of the work

    3. Distribute the catechism in time for each family to learn it

    4. Deal gently and make it easy for them to come

    5. Go to the reluctant and urge them to the work

  B. How to be effective in the work

    1. Begin with soothing, gentle words

    2. Deal with each one privately and individually

    3. Assess the level of their understanding

    4. Further test their understanding by focusing on important points

    5. Advance their understanding through further instruction

6. Test their state if we suspect they are unconverted

7. If they show they are unconverted, press home the truth of the gospel

8. Conclude the conversation with a call to further action

9. Send the people on their way with soothing words

10. If possible, give them a little charity

C. The manner of the whole conference

1. Deal with each person according to his or her particular characteristics

2. Be as humble, familiar, and plain as possible

3. Give them proof from Scripture of all we say

4. Be serious in everything, especially in the application

5. Take care with our own hearts

6. Begin with private prayer; end by praying with the people

7. Convey that we do everything only out of love for their souls

8. If necessary, and only if necessary, speak to several people at a time

9. Keep a record of everyone who comes

D. A final encouragement

General Index

honor, to be ambassador of God, 91
humiliation, 70, 85–86
humility, 64, 75, 137
hypocrisy, 36

ignorant
    instruction of, 55
    pity for, 115
impatience with reproof, 74
impenitent
    excluding or avoiding, 59
    reproving and admonishing, 58
individual soul care, 13, 19, 21, 48–49,
        104, 105, 113, 131
indwelling sin, 31, 36
inferiors and the younger, dealing
        with, 137
irreverence in the things of God, 65

Jesus Christ
    conversational preaching of, 114,
        125
    as great and good shepherd, 48
    purchased church with his own
        blood, 94
    treasury of his blessings, 47
judgment and sin, 24

Kidderminster, 14–15, 16, 18, 19–20
knowing divine truths, benefit and
        necessity of, 131
knowledge of the flock, 11

large parishes, distance between pas-
        tors and flock, 101
living in actual sins that you preach
        against in others, 32–33
Lord's Day, better spending of, 104
Lord's Supper, 54
love, for people, 66, 130, 138
lust, 53

man-pleasing disposition, 110
ministerial work
    character of, 64–67
    difficulties of, 109–12
    faithfulness in, 115
    necessity of, 112–16
    shape of, 61–64
    as slavery and drudgery, 122
    as spiritual, 65–66
    true nature of, 103
ministers
    assistance for, 49
    behavior of, 130
    covetousness of, 38, 39
    entrusted with honor of Christ,
        39–40
    example contradicts their doctrine,
        33
    falls observed by many, 38–39
    heinous aggravations of sins, 39
    idleness of, 105, 121
    labor and suffering of, 123
    as lazy and unfaithful, 38
    living in the sins that are preached
        against in others, 32–33
    must give an account, 116, 117
    as overseers, 46, 48–49, 55
    peace of conscience, 105
    poverty of, 49–50
    qualifications for, 33
    as schoolmasters, 103–4
    stewards of Christ's mysteries, 93
    time for studies, 119–20
    unfitness and unskillfulness
        among, 111
    vanity of, 121
ministry
    call to, 93
    dying to, 58
    intensity and sustainability of, 127–28

time and strength, to be laid out for God, 121

To Be a Christian: An Anglican Catechism, 141

troubled, comforting the consciences of, 58

unbelief, 36, 110–11

unconverted, instruction to, 135

ungrounded confidence in Christ, 113

union and communion with fellow laborers, 67

unsound professors, bringing to faith, 50–51

vanities of this present life, 47

visitation, 10, 20
    cost of, 19

scheduling of, 132
    See also private instruction

watchfulness, 46

weak Christians, strengthening of, 51–52

weaker capacity, being humble and plain with those of, 137

weak faith, 110–11

wealth, use of, 35

Worcestershire Association, 18, 19

works of charity, 66, 83

world, cares and business of, 91

worldliness, 52, 53

youthful, dealing with, 137

zealous for good works, 97, 143

Scripture Index